CARRIE'S CHILDREN

CARRIE'S CHILDREN

How One Mother Prepared Her Children to Become Selma's Foot Soldiers

CLARENCE T. JONES

Patrick-Turner Publishing/Nouveau Press

Published by Nouveau Press
An imprint of Patrick-Turner Publishing
2009 Brookings Lane SE.
Smyrna, Georgia 30080

Library of Congress Control Number: 2026904005

Publisher's Cataloging-in-Publication Data

Jones, Clarence T., 1953-
Carrie's children : how one mother prepared her children to become Selma's foot soldiers / Clarence T. Jones. -- First edition.

216 pages : illustrations ; 23 cm

Includes bibliographical references.
Summary: Documents one family's participation in the Selma civil rights movement from the perspective of the children who marched, centering on mother Carrie Louise Lundy's decision to prepare her nine children for activism through radical trust and courage. Author participated in both Selma to Montgomery marches, including Bloody Sunday at age twelve.

ISBN 978-1-889101-14-9 (hardcover)
ISBN 978-1-889101-15-6 (paperback)
ISBN 978-1-889101-16-3 (ebook)

1. Jones, Clarence T., 1953- --Childhood and youth. 2. Lundy, Carrie Louise. 3. Civil rights movements--Alabama--Selma--History--20th century. 4. African Americans--Civil rights--Alabama--Selma--History--20th century. 5. Selma-Montgomery Rights March (1965 : Selma, Ala.) 6. African American children--Alabama--Selma--Biography. 7. African American families--Alabama--Selma--History--20th century. 8. African American mothers--Alabama--Selma--Biography. 9. Catholic schools--Alabama--Selma--History--20th century. 10. Selma (Ala.)--Race relations--History--20th century. I. Title.

323.1196073076145

Cover design and interior by Garon Hart
Cover photograph from Jones family album

First Edition, March 2026
Printed in the United States of America

10 9 8 7 6 5 4 3 2 1

For more information, visit noveaupress.com or email info@nouveaupress.com

In memory of Carrie Louise Lundy—Mommie

CONTENTS

PREFACE

What We Carry

As a child growing up in the heart of the Jim Crow South, in Selma, Alabama, there were certain moments I could not understand. I didn't know how to resolve them. Moments like the killing of the four young girls in a Birmingham church, and George Wallace blocking Black students from entering the door of the University of Alabama. There was also the beating and trampling of young and old on the Edmund Pettus Bridge, and the killings of Viola Liuzzo, mother of five children, and Leroy Moton on the road back to Selma. And why couldn't a woman sit anywhere on the bus she wanted to?

All of these moments, and so many more, grated against what I knew to be right. My mother, Carrie, was the main source who supplied me with my values about right and wrong. I not only learned from Carrie, but from my grandmother Hettie, the Catholic Church, and the Catholic school where Carrie sent her children for their education. Every morning, I served Mass at the Convent of the Sisters of Saint Joseph and ate breakfast with them—or, I should say, *they* ate breakfast with *me*, a twelve-year-old Black boy. Nothing they ever did or said suggested to me that I was different from them or they from me, just because of our skin. In fact, they always taught that we were all people of God and that there was no fundamental distinction between us, no matter our skin hue.

But even today, with the broader perspective of adulthood, I recognize that how we look at one another and ourselves is, in fact, a choice. Do you see yourself as superior, inferior, or as God himself sees you? God asks us to love others as we love ourselves. This is the true measure of a person. While I am no longer twelve years old, I see that these same types of events and bad behaviors are on the rise. Are the adults exhibiting these behaviors today the very same young people who stood mocking and jeering at pivotal moments in the civil rights movement?

In 2003, decades after my lunches at the Convent, I began to understand the greater context that had created my childhood confusion. It took me a half century before I realized that my family had come to be part of a Catholic missionary operation in Selma, Alabama. This was not a climactic discovery, but a combination of evidence that eventually assembled into a whole picture. It was as though I was in a darkroom watching an old-fashioned photograph develop: One by one, familiar faces were taking shape from what had seemed mere shadows.

The realization started with questions that never occurred to me as a child. Why did a German-born doctor, Dr. Isabelle Dumont, practice medicine in Selma instead of a more prestigious location? How had Carrie, a young Black woman from Saint Ann Street, found herself working in such close proximity with white medical missionaries in the segregated South of the 1940s and 1950s? What had prompted the Sisters of Saint Joseph to open Saint Elizabeth Catholic School in our community?

The answers, when they finally came together, revealed a story within a story: a purposeful, orchestrated plan by Roman Catholic missionaries to minister to Selma's Black community through medicine, education, and social service. And Dr. Dumont hadn't simply chosen Selma out of the blue. She'd been sent there by Archbishop Thomas Joseph Toolen of Birmingham, who, in response to her announcement that she wanted to serve as a missionary in Africa, had informed her that there were people who needed her services only one hundred miles away.

The relationship between Dr. Dumont and Ms. Joan Mulder, her Dutch colleague, was more than professional; they were a mission team that believed in offering holistic healthcare to those for whom it was hardest to come by. Their clinic on Selma's Broad Street, the training they gave my mother, and the financial support that made it possible for us to go to Saint Elizabeth were all part of a holistic mission to combat the medical, educational, and social deficits of families locked out of mainstream support—families like mine.

My mother was the crucial bridge between this missionary project and the community it would serve. Her job as a nurse, lab technician, and midwife wasn't just work; it was ministry in the purest meaning of the word. Her expertise, cultural knowledge, and familiarity with the community were tools to translate professional medical care into something families could fully grasp. She met them where they were—not just paying attention to physical symptoms but also to other situations that influenced health.

Having this context made plain sense of the paradox that had puzzled me as a child. The same Catholic faith that led nuns to treat me with dignity and equality at the breakfast table also motivated a comprehensive mission to serve families that segregated society had abandoned. The love I experienced daily at the Convent wasn't exceptional kindness, but rather the natural expression of beliefs that saw all people as children of God, deserving equal care and opportunity.

But this understanding also brought to my attention how much essential work performed by people like Carrie remained invisible to official history. Their midwifery services, informal medical care, community support networks, and daily acts of service sustained entire neighborhoods through some of their most challenging times. Yet all of this was simultaneously crucial and unrecognized, documented only in birth records and family memories rather than in historical accounts.

The story I am about to tell is the story of one extraordinary woman and her family within this missionary context. Three people's perspectives and experiences carry the story forward: my grandmother Hettie, my mother Carrie, and myself, Clarence Jr. Carrie remains the central figure who holds the story together, whose words, actions, and spirit encapsulated unmatched compassion. Hettie's part of the story depicts the sturdy roots from which Carrie grew and blossomed. My own contribution to the narrative, as well as vignettes and insights from my siblings, display the ways Carrie's values inspired those around her to do right in the world. Yet this is far more than the tale of a grandmother, mother, and son. It is a window into the resilient perseverance and shared love of a Black community in one of the most tumultuous times in U.S. history.

Most narratives concerning the Civil Rights Movement detail famous leaders and dramatic moments. The foot soldiers who marched and the mothers who allowed them to march rarely receive proper acknowledgment. Those individuals—the foot soldiers and their mothers—their stories matter. They allow us to see how they were prepared to display such courage in the face of much adversity.

The story contained in these pages tells of how communities can cultivate potential when individuals of dissimilar backgrounds labor together toward shared goals. It is the story of how individual acts of service can have consequences that extend far beyond their immediate circumstances.

Younger generations of my family and others don't know much about what life was like during this period. These memories will disappear if we don't preserve them. Strength can be poured into the younger and next generations if we speak of these memories and past lives.

I hope to inspire young families with examples of how even in discouraging times, and amid poverty, they can raise courageous young people through everyday activities: work, education, routine, and caring for one another. My mother built courage and preparation into us not through dramatic gestures, but through daily trust and responsibility.

And most importantly, it's about what we take with us from those who heed the call to invest in our growth—the values, the knowledge, the confident vision of a lived life shaped by dedicated service, and an unyielding hope that hard work, respect for difference, and awareness of one another's humanity can and should be at the heart of how we see each other.

What follows is my effort to pay respect to that memory and to make it a source of continuous inspiration for future generations who will have their own obstacles to confront and their own opportunities to choose between love and hate, service and selfishness, hope and despair. I hope that the lessons learned in a small house surrounded by pecan trees and pink roses continue to inspire future generations.

—Clarence T. Jones

CHAPTER ONE

Where We Come From

Certain places shape you long before you understand what shape you're becoming. For me and my siblings, that place was Selma, Alabama, a city once buzzing with freight trains, factory sirens, gospel choirs, and the thick aroma of frying cornmeal cakes coming from every direction. The place where cotton fields ran into brick kilns, where ancient oaks held the memory of generations, and where the river whispered both stories and warnings.

In the early to mid-1950s and into the late 1960s, Selma was a vital industrial manufacturing town, situated on the Alabama River and the Louisville & Nashville railroad line. With a then population of thirty-two thousand, complete with thriving industry, it was the fifth-largest city in Alabama, as the nuns at Saint Elizabeth would eventually tell us. Products such as bricks, cotton, processed meats, textile goods, candy, salt, magnesium, and agricultural implements were all produced in Selma.

When walking on Mabry Street you might smell the wafting aroma of peppermint candy, or when strolling along Selma Avenue you might catch the nutty smell of the cotton gin, where cotton was made into bales. On the banks of the Alabama River, near downtown, you may be hit by the chlorine-like odor of dolomite from quarries in Shelby County, used to produce magnesium. A bit further along the river you might be hit again by the sharp pungent emission of sulfur dioxide from the brick kilns.

The town was prospering, but it was also racially divided. The movements of Black Americans were quite limited, a reality they were constantly reminded of by posted signs saying, *White Only* or *No Coloreds.* But within our community, there was life, purpose, and the kind of resilience that comes from people who understand that survival depends on taking care of one another.

More than a city, Selma was a cradle, and at its center was the woman we all called "Mommie." Our mother, Carrie, was many things: nurse, midwife, seamstress, disciplinarian, protector, cook, and confidante. But before any of those titles, she was Mommie. We always pronounced it with two clear syllables—*Mom-mee*—soft, sacred like a song. But before there was Mommie, there was the woman who shaped her: Hettie Lundy, who ruled 1410 Saint Ann Street like a queen holding court.

Hettie Lundy married at thirteen and became a mother at sixteen. She was one of fifteen siblings herself, the grand matriarch of our sprawling family tree. When Carrie Louise arrived in 1927 as Hettie's first child, she entered a world where responsibility came early, and excuses came never.

From my earliest memories, my grandmother was always working. Her hands never seemed to rest: sorting laundry at the dry cleaners, pouring whiskey shots for drop-in customers, or roasting something savory in her stove that could draw neighbors from three blocks away. She always had at least two places of employment, plus her important side gig of selling whiskey by the shot. She never attempted to hide her home business from us children. In those days, children did not concern themselves with adult business.

What I remember most about my grandmother is that she was the best cook around, making things such as fried chicken or pork chops, stovetop cornmeal hoecakes, fried corn, tomato and okra succotash, and an occasional roasted rabbit or squirrel with sweet potatoes. She allowed us children to watch as she cooked, and whenever I went to her home, the aromas of stovetop cornbread, fresh-fried corn scraped from the cob, and fried chicken, pork chops, or fish always filled the place. It was nearly impossible to leave without eating. Between her and our mother, all of us would eventually become good cooks.

Hettie never needed an alarm clock. For her, waking at 5:30 in the morning came as naturally as breathing, and by the time the rest of Saint Ann Street began to stir, she'd have already been moving for an hour. The coffee was percolating, sending its rich aroma through the small wooden house, beckoning the neighbors who'd stop by for a cup on their way to work. The first load of laundry was already soaking in the big galvanized tub on the back porch.

Carrie—the woman who would become known throughout Selma as someone who could deliver your baby, mend your injury, or feed your family—received her first lessons about service from watching Hettie navigate those early morning hours and make magic out of almost nothing.

Being the oldest child during this period meant that you were sure to grow up fast and soon have responsibilities to help raise your siblings. This was certainly true for Carrie, whose mother, Hettie, was only sixteen when Carrie was born. As Carrie's brother Willie would later tell his nieces Gwendolyn and Carolyn, "Your mother was smart enough to go to medical school, but she had to stay home and help raise us." Uncle Willie would finish college, go to medical school, and become a podiatrist, but Carrie's path would be different. Her path would be shaped by duty, love, and an early understanding that sometimes the greatest service means setting aside your own dreams for others who need you more.

Carrie would be the first of nine siblings: five boys and four girls. Like her mother, she would also give birth to five boys and four girls, although this pattern wouldn't reveal itself until years later. What mattered in those early years was learning Hettie's lessons: how to stretch a dollar until it turned tearful, how to feed whoever showed up at your door, how to work two jobs and still find energy for kindness, and how to love fiercely without ever saying the words.

The rhythm of life at 1410 Saint Ann Street became Carrie's first education. She watched Hettie balance the demands of her work at the laundry, the candy factory, and the steady stream of neighbors who appeared for a shot of whiskey or a word of advice. Carrie learned that being the matriarch meant being the one people turned to when everything else failed, and that leadership wasn't about giving orders; it was about never saying no when someone genuinely needed help. Hettie's example taught her that strength comes not from never bending, but from always getting back up to serve whoever needs you next.

These were the lessons that would later shape everything Carrie did: how she raised nine children on a nurse's salary, how she opened her door to anyone who needed care, and how she found the courage to let those children walk into history when the movement came to Selma. The foundation was laid at 1410 Saint Ann Street, by the hands of a woman who somehow knew exactly how to prepare her eldest daughter for a life of service that would touch hundreds of families across two generations.

From her kitchen window, Hettie could see the whole rhythm of her neighborhood beginning at dawn. Mr. Charlie walked down his front steps with care while carrying his lunch bucket to start his workday at the lumber mill. Mrs. Robinson stood outside her house to shake out her rug before the morning dew became too heavy. The start of the day was filled with the nonstop sound of screen doors opening and closing as people began their daily activities.

Hettie received a gentle knock at her front door, which signaled the real beginning of her day. Mrs. Sarah, who resided one block over, held a small glass container in her hand.

"Morning, Hettie. I know it's early, but you got anything for my nerves today?"

Hettie wiped her hands dry on her apron and withdrew to the back room, returning with a small flask. "Take two fingers' worth with your coffee, Sarah. No more than that."

As Hettie handed over the flask, she quietly said, "A quarter this time, Sarah." Mrs. Sarah eagerly received the container, thanked Hettie, pressed a quarter into her hand, and turned to make her way back home with her morning medicine. This was how Hettie supplemented the money she earned at the laundry and at the candy factory—not with shame or secrecy, but rather as one additional way of looking after her community, and then her family.

By 6:15, young Carrie, already dressed, appeared in the kitchen doorway, ready to help her mother before leaving for school. At thirteen, she was accustomed to the morning routine she'd known all her life. She'd already looked in on her younger siblings, folded the clothes that had dried overnight, and was beginning to set up breakfast for whoever needed feeding.

"Carrie, honey, come start on this corn bread while I get your brothers moving," Hettie called as she pulled ingredients out of the cupboard. Carrie understood without explanation; the boys would need breakfast before they headed out to school, and there was never enough time to do everything that needed doing.

As usual, the kitchen at 1410 Saint Ann Street was full with its morning sounds: the scraping as Carrie measured out cornmeal, the hissing sizzle as the batter met the hot cast-iron skillet, voices murmuring in the far back and middle rooms as Hettie's sons were beginning to rise. Through it all, Carrie was watching her mother's hands and without knowing exactly when, she had learned how much salt to add, when to whip the batter, when the skillet was hot enough, and how long before it would be fried.

"Mrs. Hettie? You in there?" came another voice at the front door. It was James from a couple of blocks over.

"Come on through, James. Coffee's ready."

James stood in the kitchen doorway, hat in hand. "Thank you, ma'am. Baby teething, up all night. Wife sent me to find whether you had anything might help."

Hettie wiped her hands on a towel and crossed the room to the wooden cabinet beside the stove. From several small bottles and jars, she chose one filled with clear liquid. "Rub just a pinch on her gums. Not too much, now. This'll put her to sleep, but it'll stop that pain."

"What do I owe you?"

"Bring me some of those late tomatoes from your garden when they come in."

This was the system of those who lived on Saint Ann Street, where Hettie coordinated the exchange of favors and kindness among neighbors. She made sure everyone got what they needed. Money was exchanged when there was money, trade when there wasn't, but there was always an understanding that helping your neighbors was how you survived.

By seven o'clock, the Lundy house was fully active. Carrie's younger brothers would stumble toward the kitchen for breakfast, everyone getting ready for their own school day while Hettie prepared for her morning at the laundry. Each morning they'd leave the house and walk down Saint Ann like they owned it. These morning walks would end at the corner where Small Avenue met Broad, with Hettie heading toward the white section of town to work in other people's kitchens and laundries, and Carrie and her siblings continuing toward their school. Before she'd part ways with Carrie, Hettie would always give the same reminder.

"Remember," Hettie would say, while adjusting Carrie's collar or smoothing her hair, "you're a Lundy wherever you go. Act like it."

For Carrie, Hettie's daily reminder was to keep the family name respected in every place she visited. The words Hettie shared with Carrie formed the basis of everything she would achieve in life. These achievements sprung from her knowledge that a person's identity extends beyond their individual self because they belong to a bigger entity that requires their excellent representation. People needed to understand that service is about dedication, and it defines their daily purpose; service isn't just an option for flexible scheduling.

Knox Academy was the school where Carrie spent her days learning reading, writing, and home economics. But her real education was already happening in the mornings, afternoons, and evenings at 1410 Saint Ann Street, watching her mother somehow know exactly how to hold together not just her own family, but half the neighborhood besides.

Everyone in the neighborhood knew the real magic happened when Hettie started cooking. Not just the everyday feeding of nine children and whoever else appeared at dinnertime, but the Sunday cooking that filled 1410 Saint Ann Street with aromas so rich they had weight and substance.

Carrie would always position herself at the kitchen table where she could watch everything: the way Hettie seasoned the cast-iron skillet with just enough grease, how she knew when the oil was hot enough for chicken by the sound it made when she flicked water into it, and the precise moment the cornbread needed turning to get that perfect golden crust.

"Hand me that pepper, baby," Hettie would say to Carrie, never looking up from the chicken she was flouring. Her hands moved with the confidence of someone who'd been feeding people since she was barely more than a child herself. "Not too much, now—just enough to wake it up."

Hettie knew the entire small kitchen floor so well that she navigated through it with the same precision as a professional dancer who had mastered all the dance steps. She carried out each task with focus and purpose; almost without looking, she went from the stove to the sink and then to the wooden table where she rolled out biscuits. Her routine followed its natural sequence without interruptions or waste, with everything moving at its own pace until the group was gathered around the table.

"Why did you put the corn in cold water first, Mama?" Carrie asked as she watched Hettie prepare fresh corn for frying.

"Easier to scrape clean off the cob." Hettie demonstrated, using the back of a knife. "See how it comes off in whole kernels instead of all mashed up and milky? That's how you get fried corn that tastes like something instead of just mush."

These weren't formal lessons—Hettie was too busy for that—but Carrie caught on quickly. How to know if chicken is done cooking by the color of the juice that comes out when you prick it with a fork. When to add okra to the tomatoes so they won't get slimy. The secret to hoecakes that didn't fall apart or get hard was mixing cornmeal with just enough hot water to hold it together and cooking it quickly on a very hot griddle until the batter danced when it landed.

"Cooking ain't just about feeding people," Hettie said one Sunday afternoon as she and Carrie worked together preparing dinner for the usual crowd of family and neighbors. "Good food, made with good intentions and a good heart, is never mistaken. People can always taste if you care about them or not; it's in the taste and appearance of the food."

The proof was in the response of people. Children who lived several blocks away would somehow show up in Hettie's kitchen around dinnertime, lured by smells that promised more than just food. Neighbors would come along with small gifts—a few greens from their garden, a generous piece of fatback, some late peaches—and always know they'd leave with more than they brought.

Hunters would sometimes gift Hettie a rabbit or a squirrel, and when she cooked them, she treated the small portions of meat like store bought delicacies. She would enhance the meals by adding savory spices and vegetables until she had a meal that satisfied everyone at the table. Sweet potatoes roasted alongside the meat would cause the outer edges to turn golden brown with caramelized sugar.

"Never let anyone leave your table hungry if you can help it," she told Carrie as they watched yet another neighbor's child clean his plate and look hopefully toward the stove. "There's always a way to make it go a little more if you use your head."

This was how Carrie learned that feeding people was both a practical skill and a spiritual calling. That the kitchen was where love became tangible. That knowing how to take almost nothing and turn it into something that nourished both body and soul was one of the most important things a person could learn.

Years later, when Carrie stood in her own kitchen at 1421 Sylvan Street feeding nine children on a nurse's salary, she'd move with the same purposeful grace her mother had shown her. She embodied the truth that meals were far more than nutrition; they were to bring people together, to demonstrate that they mattered, by giving them something like abundance even in a time of scarcity.

The walk from 1421 Sylvan Street to our grandmother's at 1410 Saint Ann Street took about ten minutes if you hurried, fifteen if you stopped to speak to Mrs. Willie Mae or anyone else you met along the way like Mommie had taught us to do. But when carrying one of Mommie's requests to Hettie, that walk could feel like an hour, especially when you weren't sure in what kind of mood your grandmother might be.

"Go ask Mama Hettie for some meal and a dozen eggs," Mommie would say, giving me or one of my sisters or brothers a small scrap of paper with her careful handwriting. "Say to her I'll pay her back on Saturday."

We all knew the drill, but knowing it and feeling okay with it were two different things. Hettie's responses were as irregular as summer weather in Alabama—sometimes sunny, sometimes stormy, but always unforgettable.

The day I started to run these errands was one of those times when Hettie's words landed more painfully than usual. I knocked on the screen door while clutching Mommie's note asking for flour and sugar as I waited for her to emerge from the back of the house.

"What you want, boy?" she inquired through the screen, wiping her hands on her apron.

"Mommie sent me after some flour and sugar. She wrote it down right here." I waved the paper like evidence in my defense.

Hettie pushed open the screen door and took the note, reading it slowly. Then she looked at me with those eyes that saw straight through to whatever you were thinking.

"What does your Mama think I am, the A&P grocery?" she said, loud enough for the neighbors across the street to hear. "Every other day somebody coming over here wanting this, wanting that. I got my own mouths to feed."

My face burned with embarrassment. At nine years old, I didn't understand that this was Hettie's way of making sure we knew the value of what she was giving, nor did I grasp that her complaints were theater performed for our education. All I knew was that I felt ashamed for asking, and I started backing away from the door.

"Yes ma'am," I mumbled, already turning to leave. "I'll tell Mommie you can't."

That's when her voice cracked like a whip across the evening air. "Boy! Get your ass back here and get what your mother sent you for!"

Like a rabbit, I stopped dead in my tracks, with my breath caught in my chest. I turned around slowly and walked back to where she stood in the doorway. Her expression had changed from irritation to something that might have been amusement.

"I didn't say I wasn't going to give it to you, did I?" She was already heading over to her pantry. "I just said your mama treats me like the corner store. That don't mean I won't take care of my daughter and her children."

She disappeared into the kitchen and came back with a five-pound sack of flour and a small bag of sugar. Then, without being asked, she added a Mason jar of her fig preserves and a small paper sack that smelled like her famous tea cakes.

"Tell Carrie these tea cakes are for you children, not for her to save for company." She pressed the bundle into my arms. "And let her know it's alright for paying back, but she should learn to ask me earlier in the week instead of when her cupboards are already empty."

The walk back felt unlike the walk there. My arms were laden with offerings and then some, but I was learning something new: For Hettie, the complaining had been part of the gift. It was her way of telling us how help always came at a cost and that being family meant keeping each other from going hungry, even when it meant sacrificing yourself.

As I gave everything to Mommie and related Hettie's words, she only smiled and shook her head. "Mama's taken care of folks for so long, she can't remember how to say yes without a fuss in between. Don't mind her complaints any. Just listen to what she does."

In the many decades since, versions of this scene repeated dozens of times, as different children came with different requests. It was my sister Joan asking for cornmeal one week, my twin brother Fred needing eggs the next, one of us sent for "just a few dollars until payday." And always the same response: complaint followed by generosity, lecture followed by love, words that stung followed by actions that healed.

We were taught to knock on the door of 1410 Saint Ann Street with respect for what we were asking, knowing why it might be a burden on our grandmother and having confidence that we'd never leave empty-handed. These weren't just errands; they were lessons in how families work, how communities survive, and how love gets expressed through service even when it comes wrapped in sharp words.

On Sunday mornings at 1410 Saint Ann Street, the day started before the chickens. By 5:30, Hettie was moving about the house with a silent purposefulness that came easily to any woman who understood that it took precise timing and divine intervention to organize not only herself but also nine children for an early church service.

The ritual never varied. She'd start by heating water in the big pot on the stove: for baths, youngest children first, then oldest, so they could each take turns getting clean and smelling like the Octagon soap she used for everything from scrubbing clothes to scrubbing kids. Then there was the laying out of church clothes and the sweeping inspection of each item to detect rips, stains, or missing buttons that could bring shame upon the family name.

"Sunday morning is when people are going to see who you really are," she'd tell Carrie as they pressed the children's clothes with the heavy iron heated on the stove. "Don't matter how poor we are during the week. On Sunday, we dress up and look like we got some sense and some pride."

At 8:30, the Lundy family of 1410 Saint Ann Street would march out like a tiny, impressive little army. Hettie took the lead in her best dress, usually dark blue with faint little white flowers, hair pinned under a hat she'd worn to church for longer than anyone could remember. Behind her there were nine children in descending order of height, all scrubbed and pressed and warned about the dreadful things that would happen to them if they misbehaved in the Lord's house.

The walk to Green Street Baptist Church was twenty minutes, but it seemed like a parade. Every third or fourth step, it seemed, someone would call out, "Morning, Sister Lundy!" or "Them children look nice for a change today, Hettie!" She'd nod and smile, taking the compliments as her due, yet she wouldn't slow down. Church began promptly at 9:30, and the Lundy family was never tardy.

Sitting inside Green Street Baptist, just being seen all the way from the deacon's stand gave Hettie stature. Folks trusted her with more than just sitting among the choir on first Sunday or bringing around the offering basket. People came to see her when something was going wrong in their families, when a child in a particular household needed to be set straight, and when someone was struggling, barely holding on, needing help they didn't want to ask for in public.

Before church, Mrs. James would come to the usher's room and whisper, "Sister Lundy, you think you could have a word with my oldest boy? He's been running with older ones I don't know, and he won't listen to me." Hettie would nod once, accepting the trust and fixing the matter in her mind to be settled after service. And that boy who wouldn't listen to his mother would suddenly find himself answering to Sister Lundy and shaping up without understanding how it happened.

During church, she sat in the third pew from the front, all three children arranged by age along the bench beside her. She sang hymns with a strong alto that could be heard three rows back, and her "Amen" at the preacher's good points sailed over the sanctuary like a cannon. She had walked with the Lord longer than some of the older members had been breathing.

But when church let out, Hettie Lundy really started talking. Families gathered outside on the church steps to hear the week's news, and Hettie moved among them, inspecting elderly members she'd noticed looking tired during service, helping one of them back inside, making a mental note of children who seemed paper-thin, families she'd heard were struggling.

"Mrs. Washington," she'd call out to the widow who'd lost her husband last month, "I cooked too much cornbread this week. Do you mind doing me a favor by taking some of it off my hands?"

This was fiction, everyone knew, because Hettie never made too much of anything. But Mrs. Washington would accept the gift with exactly the courtesy intended and would know that this is how love went in their neighborhood. Aid arrived in stories that allowed people to maintain dignity while also accessing the support they required.

When the Lundy family got home, Hettie would have already dedicated herself to twelve tiny acts of service for the next week. A visit to someone ill and recovering. A pot of soup for a family whose father had lost his job. A quiet word with a wayward teenager. A couple of dollars slipped to someone whose lights were about to go out.

"Why do you keep taking on everybody else's problems?" Carrie asked her mother one Sunday afternoon as they prepared dinner for the usual family members and neighbors who stopped by after church.

Hettie glanced up from the chicken she was frying, her expression serious. "'Cause that's what we're here for, baby. To take care of each other. When you've got more than you need, share it. When you have strength, you help the weak. That's not tackling problems—that's just being human."

This was the template Carrie would follow for the rest of her own life. There was a lesson there in what it meant to be a leader: Leadership was power through service, and strength was defined by lifting people up. Sunday morning was not an end but a prelude to a week that challenged you to prove that your faith is more than just something you declare.

By the time Carrie was fourteen, she moved about 1410 Saint Ann Street like a second mother, and everyone, including Hettie, had come to depend on it. The younger children sought her out whenever they wanted anything, and she responded with a blend of tender and stern resolution that appeared to come to her as naturally as breathing.

"Carrie, baby, come in here and help me with these children," Hettie would call from her back room where she was attempting to ready the younger three—Willie, Isaac, and John—for the day. It was never really a request; it was always more like a signal that the day's work had begun, and everyone had their role to play.

There Carrie would stand with her arms already full of those things children just have to have: clean socks, hair ribbons, and the washcloth for faces that had managed somehow to get dirty between wake-up time and breakfast. She'd labor by her mother's side with the efficiency of one who had been doing this work since she was barely able to lean on the washbasin herself.

"Hold still, Isaac," she'd say to her brother, working a comb into his hair as he squirmed and grumbled. "You want to go to school looking like you stuck a finger in a light socket?"

The patience she had with her younger siblings was amazing, given the fact she was barely more than a child herself. When her little sister Marzetta wailed over being asked to wear a dress she had outgrown over the summer, Carrie would manage to let down the hem or add some strip of contrasting fabric that made it look like it was meant to be that way. When baby Larry didn't want to eat his breakfast, she'd make airplane noises with the spoon until he opened his mouth just so his big sister would stop with the nonsense.

"You're good with them," Hettie said one morning, watching Carrie braid Lizzie's hair neatly into plaits. "Got the touch for knowing what the kids need before they know to ask."

"They're not too complicated," Carrie said, tying the second braid up with a strip of fabric. "They just want someone to know that people are looking after them."

This was the beginning of Carrie's education in the art of mothering—not the biological fact of having children, but the daily practice of keeping them fed, clean, and safe, and making sure they felt loved even when resources were scarce and patience was running thin. She also learned how to stretch a pot of grits by adding more water and claiming that it was "creamy style." She found that if you sang while you braided hair, children would sit still longer. She finally realized that the really creative way of stopping a fight between siblings was to give them something they had to do as a team!

After school, while other babies were playing in the streets, Carrie would come straight home to assist with making ready for the afternoon's work. There was always laundry to fold, someone who needed help with lessons, a baby in need of changing or feeding. She would work beside Hettie, learning on the job and gathering wisdom that would serve her well when she had nine children of her own.

Though Carrie was skilled at her household responsibilities, she didn't always enjoy them. "Mama, why can't the boys help more with the little ones?" she asked one afternoon as she stirred a pot of beans while bouncing baby Larry on her hip. "Willie's strong enough to carry them around. And Bertha is only three years younger than me—why can't she help out more?"

Hettie raised her head from the shirt she was darning. "Boys got other work to do. Willie needs to be learning about how to support a family. And Bertha's time will come when she has to help more with the younger ones. You're the oldest, so you should be the one learning how to take care of children. That's just how it is."

It was 1941, and the world still appeared to be splitting along lines that were as immutable as the sunrise. Men's work and women's work; what children could hope for from life depending on whether they were born male or female, Black or white; the realization that some dreams were realistic and others were pipe dreams that families like theirs couldn't afford.

But given those constraints, Carrie was learning skills that would prove invaluable—how to run a home when everyone had needs but resources were finite. How to be hard enough to keep order but soft enough to keep a child's spirit alive. How to make time for teaching and tenderness when the day was so full of the things that had to be done.

"The trick to it," Hettie explained to her one night as they sat mending clothes with the lamplight burning, "is to remember that looking after folks is holy work. Whether it's changing diapers, fixing supper, or spending time with the sick child who knows only one word: 'more'—when you do it with love and to make things better for the child, in God's eyes, you're doing holy work."

These weren't profound philosophical discussions about the meaning of life. They were practical talks between a mother and daughter who both realized that life was going to make great demands on them, and that the measure of a person was how gracefully they made those sacrifices. Carrie was learning to find joy and fulfillment in something that would never make her famous, never make her rich, but would help define the lives of anyone she crossed paths with.

Years later, when people expressed amazement that Carrie could raise nine children while working full time as a nurse and midwife, she would think back to these afternoons at 1410 Saint Ann Street. The lessons in efficiency, patience, and finding joy in service. The realization that strength wasn't about never getting tired. It was about getting up and doing what you had to do, even when you were tired. Especially when you were tired.

It was a Tuesday morning late in the summer of 1945 when the letter from Good Samaritan Hospital arrived. Three months out of high school, Carrie had been working at various odd jobs around the neighborhood—helping Mrs. James with her washing, minding children for mothers who worked in white folks' kitchens, anything that would bring in a few dollars to supplement Hettie's housekeeping pay. But within Carrie there were aspirations for something more.

"What's that official-looking envelope?" Hettie asked as Carrie pulled the letter out of her back pocket and turned it over in her palms.

"It's from the hospital. About their nursing program." Carrie's tone was even, cautious. They'd spoken of this possibility. Carrie had heard about an opportunity to be trained as a nurse, discussed it with her mother, and reached out for more information. But talking and having it arrive in your hands were two entirely different things.

Hettie wiped her hands on her apron and held out her hand. "Let me see it."

The letter was formal but encouraging. Applications were being accepted for Good Samaritan Hospital's Training School for Nursing by and for Colored Girls. The program would offer room, board, and training in exchange for work at the hospital during the lessons. Graduates would be qualified to work as registered nurses serving the colored community of Selma and surrounding areas. This was a groundbreaking development since Jim Crow laws restricted who was allowed to work as a nurse.

"Room and board," read Hettie aloud. "That means one less mouth to feed here."

That was practical thinking, but there was something else in her mother's voice Carrie picked up on: a note of possibility that hadn't been sounded when they talked about this as some far-off dream.

"I could still even be of some help at home," Carrie said quickly. "The hospital's not that far. I could drop by after work, watch the kids . . ."

"No." Hettie's voice was firm. "If you're going to do this thing, you do it proper. You can't be a nurse halfway, worrying about what's happening at home every minute. These kids will learn how to get along without you. And Bertha's here to help out in your place."

The reality was, Hettie had been brooding over this moment for months. She'd watched Carrie move throughout the house with exceptional competence, taking charge of younger children and showing natural instincts for detecting illness and injury and providing care to those who needed it. The girl had two special gifts: She could heal naturally, and she learned very quickly.

Hettie took a seat across from Carrie at the kitchen table and asked her a question. "You sure you want this? It's not going to be easy. Taking care of people in a hospital is hard, and some of those white people who run the place might not treat you like they should."

"I'm sure, Mama. I want to know how to actually help people, not just take wild guesses as to what might be comforting."

Together over the next hour, mother and daughter completed the application. Hettie wrote her answers to the questions about Carrie's education and health status and personal background using her precise handwriting. When they reached the section about family responsibilities, they both paused. "You can put that you help take care of younger siblings," Hettie said at last. "They want to know that you already get what it means to care for people."

The application was in the mail that afternoon, and for three weeks they waited. Carrie worked multiple jobs while the entire house sensed their upcoming change, though they were not ready for it.

When Carrie got an acceptance letter, and then another letter with directions to come to Good Samaritan Hospital on September 15 for the start of training, it hit her all at once. Carrie Louise Lundy was going to be a nurse.

"You remember what I taught you about doing for people," Hettie said the night before Carrie left for the hospital. They observed the house through open windows, settling on a front porch and listening to some familiar neighborhood sounds as the community was winding down for the night. "It's not just a question of knowing what medicine to give or how to bandage a wound. It's about seeing that person as a human being who has more than just his or her body to be fixed."

"Yes ma'am. I'll remember."

"And you remember that this family's name is to be borne by you. Everything you do, you make us proud."

The next morning, Carrie walked out of 1410 Saint Ann Street carrying a small suitcase and wearing her finest dress. Behind her, eight brothers and sisters looked on from the front porch as their big sister walked into a future that none of them could quite imagine.

It was the start of Carrie's journey from being Hettie's child to becoming her own woman—one who would remain committed to family and service while knowing she was capable of lifting others up in ways that would ripple through hundreds of lives over decades. Everything that would come later rested on the foundation laid on Saint Ann Street.

Within three months of starting her nursing program, Carrie had settled into the rhythm of Good Samaritan Hospital. The days were grueling and seemingly endless: lectures in anatomy and physiology in the morning, practice rounds on the wards in the afternoon, evenings spent studying by lamplight. But for the first time in her life, she was learning skills that felt like they coincided with the intelligence she'd always possessed but never known quite what to do with.

"Miss Lundy," Sister Louis Bertrand called one afternoon as Carrie was finishing up changing beds in the men's ward. "Could you stay a moment?"

The head administrator of Good Samaritan was a formidable type—short and stout, but efficient, and known for not wasting time or words. When she called you out and told you to stay after, it was either something very good or quite the opposite, with not much in between.

"Yes, Sister," Carrie replied.

"How have you found the program thus far?"

"I'm learning a lot, Sister. More than I expected to learn."

Sister Louis Bertrand nodded approvingly. "Your teachers indicate that you're really good with patients. They respond well to you."

"I just try to treat them the way I'd want to be treated if I was sick and far from home."

"That's more unusual than you might realize. Most students learn these technical skills but never develop an intuition for what sick people need." The nun hesitated, scrutinizing Carrie's expression. "I'm telling you this because I want you to know that we're watching your progress with interest. There may be opportunities for students who show both the competence and compassion you have shown so far."

Carrie wasn't entirely sure what that meant, but she tucked it away in the section of her mind where she kept things like notes and half-remembered items that might be useful later. She was just really starting to grasp how life at Good Samaritan worked on two planes: the surface track of the school's formally prescribed program, and then the private network of relationships and opportunities that opened up for students who showed themselves to be reliable and trustworthy.

As she walked home to Saint Ann Street that night—she'd continued to come home twice a week to assist Hettie with the younger children—Carrie felt something new, something she had never felt before. The pride not just of a job well done, but of a purpose beyond the duties of family. She was becoming a person who could make a difference in the world, whose abilities would be sought out and treasured.

"How's nursing school going?" Hettie asked as they worked on preparing supper for whoever might appear that evening.

"Good, Mama. Hard, but good. I feel I'm cut out for this sort of work."

Hettie smiled a smile that said she'd known this all along and was happy to know her daughter had discovered it for herself. "Always did have healing hands. You were always the one the other kids came to when they hurt themselves, even when you were little."

What neither of them could have known that evening was that change was already on its way to Selma in the person of a German doctor who would soon present her plans to serve the colored community, or that Sister Louis Bertrand was already considering which of her nursing students might be ready for responsibilities for which none yet had an inkling.

The stage was being set for everything that would come after: her partnership with a German-born, Catholic missionary physician named

Dr. Dumont, her years of service as both nurse and midwife, and the house on Sylvan Street that would become a center of healing and hope. But for the moment, it was enough to know that Carrie Louise Lundy was becoming just what she was intended to be: a woman whose intelligence and compassion would enrich hundreds of lives in the decades ahead.

CHAPTER TWO

The Power to Heal

The knock on Sister Louis Bertrand's office door came one Tuesday morning in March 1944, when the daffodils were first poking their green shoots through the earth around Good Samaritan Hospital and when the war in Europe felt both far away and chillingly close to Selma. Sister Louis glanced up from her paperwork to find a tall, serious woman looking down at her with kind eyes, yet the undeniable presence of someone used to being the smartest person in most rooms.

"Hello, I am Dr. Isabelle Schmitz-Dumont," the woman said in accented English that carried remnants of her homeland, Germany. "I think that Archbishop Toolen may have told you I would come to visit with you."

Sister Louis put down her pen and eyed her visitor. She had indeed heard from Birmingham that a medical missionary was on the way to Selma, but the information had been sketchy. What she saw before her was a woman who appeared able to withstand whatever challenges might come her way while serving the colored community of West Central Alabama.

"Please, sit down, Dr. Dumont. I've been expecting you."

What ensued was a conversation that would alter the course of medical treatment options for Black families throughout the region, though neither woman could have foreseen what they were setting into motion. Dr. Dumont discussed her travels from Germany, through medical school in the United States, and on to her appeal to Archbishop Thomas Joseph Toolen of Birmingham, Alabama about missionary work in Africa.

"It occurred to the Archbishop that I didn't need to go halfway around the world if there were people nearby begging for health care," Dr. Dumont said with a wry smile. "He said to me, 'We are just one hundred miles away from Selma, and this service is very much necessary here.'"

Sister Louis nodded. She had run Good Samaritan Hospital for three years, enough time to know that a single hospital could not serve all the medical needs of the colored community in Dallas County and beyond. The prospect of a focused clinic, under the leadership of someone like Dr. Dumont, was exactly what she had prayed for.

Dr. Dumont had not come to Selma alone. Her missionary partner, Ms. Joan Mulder from Holland, had joined her in this work of serving the colored community. Where Dr. Dumont brought medical expertise, Ms. Joan, who shared the same deep commitment to their mission, would contribute administrative skills.

"I'm going to open a clinic on Broad Street," Dr. Dumont went on. "But I'll need a nurse to help me. Someone who knows the community, who can help bridge knowledge of medicine and public health with people's real lives. Sister, who is your best and brightest nursing student that you could recommend for this position?"

Sister Louis didn't hesitate. "Carrie Louise Lundy. She's terrific—technically competent but, more important, she's instinctively attuned to what sick people require. And how patients respond to her—I've seldom seen that."

"Could I meet her?"

Less than an hour after that, Carrie was sitting across from Dr.

Dumont in Sister Louis's office, still wearing the same hospital-issued clothes and trying to process just what was being offered to her. The German doctor scrutinized Carrie the way she herself would a difficult medical case.

"Sister Bertrand says you're her best student," Dr. Dumont said. "But I'm more looking for what you tell me. What made you want to be a nurse?"

Carrie had been questioned about this before, but there was something about Dr. Dumont's clear-eyed gaze that made her want to be more honest than she'd ever dared.

"As a child, I saw my mother taking care of everybody on Saint Ann Street. Her own family, yes, but anybody who needed help. She was not a medical professional but had hands that healed and a heart that didn't know how to look away from human pain. I want to be able to do what she did, but with the science behind it, so that I can actually help people get better."

Dr. Dumont nodded slowly. "Without compassion, medical knowledge is valueless. Compassion without medicine is risky business. You seem to know that both are needed."

"Yes ma'am, I do."

"The work won't be easy. We're serving people who often can't pay very much, if anything at all. We are going to see conditions that may have been preventable had there been available access to care. We will encounter resistance from some segments of the white community who do not believe that people of color should receive the same quality medical attention. Are you prepared for that?"

Carrie thought of Hettie, and of the neighbors who came to their door seeking help that was nowhere else to be had; she thought of the little children in her community who suffered from diseases which correct medical care would have prevented or cured.

"I'm prepared, Dr. Dumont. That's what I want to do with my life."

The bond that was forged on that first day would last for over twenty years and reach hundreds of families in West Central Alabama. Dr. Dumont would give the medical knowledge and tools; Carrie would be the bridge between professional healthcare and community necessity. This arrangement became far more for all of them than they might have ever imagined on that March morning.

But first there was training to do. Dr. Dumont arranged for Carrie to receive in-depth, one-on-one training, above and beyond the basics found in nursing school. Carrie was immersed in courses in anatomy, physiology, microbiology, pharmacology, and nutrition, but she was also developing other practical skills that would be especially important in a clinic that served a community pushed to society's margins by racial and economic factors. Carrie would be taught how to draw blood and run laboratory tests and help with minor surgical procedures. She would learn how to differentiate between symptoms that needed immediate attention and those that could be managed with careful monitoring.

"I'm going to teach you everything I can," Dr. Dumont told Carrie on the nurse's first day working in the clinic on Broad Street. "The people we're serving deserve the best care we can give them, and that means you need to deliver care on a scale greater than most nurses might have been expected to perform."

The clinic itself was humble: three rooms in a narrow building directly across the street from a small bakery where, in years to come, Carrie's future children would stop for bread for sandwiches for their daily lunches. But Dr. Dumont had equipped the office with everything needed to provide full medical care: examination tables, basic surgical tools, a small laboratory for bloodwork and other tests, and a pharmacy stocked with medications that were often impossible for colored patients to obtain elsewhere in Selma.

"Ms. Joan will work directly with us," Dr. Dumont told Carrie during her first week at the clinic. "She takes a lot of the correspondence with supporters, manages our supplies and equipment, and assists in patient coordination when I'm called for emergencies."

Ms. Joan was quieter than Dr. Dumont but equally dedicated. Carrie quickly learned to appreciate Ms. Joan's methodical approach to organization and her genuine care for every patient who walked through their doors. On days when the work ran late, Ms. Joan would often drive Carrie home in her creamy beige MG convertible. The two women would develop a friendship that bridged their diverse backgrounds through their shared commitment to service.

Carrie adapted fast, receiving not just the technical skills but also Dr. Dumont's philosophy of patient care. Every person who walked through the clinic's door was treated with the same dignity and attention, regardless of their ability to pay or the color of their skin. Histories were painstakingly recorded, symptoms discussed earnestly, and treatments described in terms the patients could understand.

"Medicine is not just about diagnosing and treating disease," Dr. Dumont explained as they geared up for their first full day of seeing patients. "It's about seeing each person as a whole human being with fears and hopes and family responsibilities that affect their health in ways that don't show up in textbooks."

That philosophy guided everything Carrie did, both in the clinic and, before long, as a midwife serving families across the community. Her medical care revolved around the conviction that healing required more than medical knowledge: It demanded a clear vision and an understanding of the people in front of you, how they lived, their circumstances, and care that fit their actual lives rather than idealized situations.

Within six months of opening, the Broad Street Clinic was the heart of medical treatment for Selma's colored populace. Word spread quickly that there was a new clinic on Broad Street where you could receive medical care from a real doctor who actually cared, and that the nurse who worked there was one of their own—someone who looked like them, lived like them, came from a family like theirs, and who understood their circumstances and their needs. The news traveled along the network of churches, barbershops, corner stores, and cafés. The small clinic soon attracted a stream of patients: children needing vaccinations, adults managing chronic conditions, and families wanting preventative care that previously had been out of reach.

Each morning on her way to work, Carrie walked with a new sense of purpose. This was not just a job. It was a calling that relied upon both her intelligence and compassion in the service of her community. And at the end of every day, walking back home amid the familiar sights and sounds of industrial Selma, she would know that she did something to make a difference in people's lives.

But the clinic was just the start. Before long, Dr. Dumont would approach Carrie with an opportunity that would extend the young nurse's healing into the most sacred moments of family life: bringing new life into the world and assisting mothers through what could sometimes be one of the lowest points in their lives.

At the end of every day, Carrie would walk home from the clinic on Broad Street to 1410 Saint Ann Street, still her place of residence alongside Hettie and some of her younger siblings, whom she continued to care for. But the walk gave her time to process the day's work, to reflect on the patients she'd seen and the treatments they'd received. Before long, she herself would be walking that stretch with Clarence Jones,* the scholarly young man who would become her husband. And soon, with financial help from Dr. Dumont, the young couple would be able to buy their own house on Sylvan Street. But for now, the rhythm of her days was moving between the medical mission and the family foundation on Saint Ann Street.

Carrie arrived at the clinic every morning at 7:30, unlocked the door, and hung up her things to prepare herself for whatever the day would bring. On some days it was the basics: taking blood pressure readings for older patients, treating minor cuts and infections, giving vaccine shots to children whose parents finally found a place to administer them. Other days brought emergencies that tested everything Dr. Dumont had taught her.

"Carrie, I need you to prepare the examination room quickly," Dr. Dumont called one Tuesday morning as she hurried in through the front door. "Mrs. Patterson is bringing her youngest boy—high fever for three days and now he's having trouble breathing."

---

* In this chapter, I refer to my father, Clarence Jones Sr., simply as Clarence Jones. At this point in the story, he has no children, so he is not yet "Senior."

When Mrs. Patterson came with her four-year-old son, Carrie had everything prepared. The child was limp, his breath rapid and shallow, his little body on fire with fever. Dr. Dumont examined him swiftly but thoroughly while Carrie took his temperature and pulse, both women working with the kind of coordinated efficiency that comes from months of practicing together.

"Pneumonia," Dr. Dumont whispered to Carrie. "We must begin treatment right now."

What followed was a delicate negotiation between medical necessity and economic reality. The medicine the child needed was costly, and Mrs. Patterson earned money as a domestic worker in white people's homes for a pittance that barely paid her rent or fed herself and five children.

"Dr. Dumont, I can pay you something every week," Mrs. Patterson said, her worry and pride evident in her tight voice. "I can't afford to pay it all at once."

"Mrs. Patterson," Dr. Dumont gently suggested to her, "your son must have this medicine immediately. We'll discuss payment later. Right now, we're just trying to make him better."

Carrie watched similar scenes play out with patients every day. Dr. Dumont was never willing to let someone's economic situation get in the way of getting the care they needed. At times, the patients paid in cash; other times, in installment payments spread over months or with goods from their garden or services like house painting or repairs. The clinic existed through this patchwork of payment methods, with some contributions from Dr. Dumont's funds and, intermittently, support from donors who believed in her mission.

But Carrie was also finding out that recovery meant more than simply addressing immediate health concerns. It meant learning about the full context of people's lives: the working conditions that caused injuries, housing situations with air quality that contributed to respiratory problems, and limited access to nutritious food which influenced children's development.

"Mrs. Williams," Carrie said to a woman who was in for the third time that month. The baby in Mrs. Williams's arms had incessant stomach troubles, and the woman was desperate for a solution. "Tell me what you're feeding him."

But a subsequent conversation showed that the baby was getting watered-down formula because Mrs. Williams could not afford enough to provide full-strength feeding. Instead of just treating malnutrition, Dr. Dumont looked beyond the exam room and pursued a more holistic solution. The doctor arranged for the clinic to sell baby formula at cost, and Carrie took time coaching Mrs. Williams on danger signs and when to bring the baby back for follow-ups.

"You're turning into more than a nurse," Dr. Dumont remarked one evening as she and Carrie were completing the last patient visit of the day. "You're really a necessary bridge between medical care and community care. That's a rare skill."

The two women's relationship was taking on a significance neither of them had anticipated. Dr. Dumont brought medical expertise and resources, but Carrie had something just as valuable: an intuition about how they could actually make modern medicine function in the everyday realities of their patients' lives. Carrie knew which families would require payment plans, which patients would be too ashamed to seek assistance unless their conditions reached a critical stage, and which children were displaying signs of trouble that might escape the notice of their parents.

The clinic had a small but efficient staff. There was Dr. Dumont, Ms. Joan, and Carrie, and then there was Mrs. Ida Bennett. Mrs. Ida was a matronly Selma resident who had previous experience in medical work, including some assistant duties at Good Samaritan Hospital, and who proved of great assistance in getting the clinic running smoothly through her administrative skills.

"Mrs. Ida knows everyone in this neighborhood," Dr. Dumont said, watching as she took phone calls and rapidly scheduled appointments while advising a concerned mother about her child's persistent cough. "She's got a kind of practical wisdom that they don't teach you at medical school."

Mrs. Ida became both confidante and friend to Carrie, someone who knew the demands of medical practice and the value of treating each patient with dignity despite their circumstances.

By the spring of 1945, as summer grew nearer, the clinic was becoming renowned. But the same could not be said for demands on Carrie's time and abilities. Dr. Dumont had started talking about growing their services, about training Carrie to add more procedures that would make it possible for them to offer even more comprehensive care to the community.

"There is something else I want to talk to you about," Dr. Dumont said one afternoon while cleaning up after a particularly busy day. "Something that could make a huge difference to the women and families we support."

Carrie glanced up from rubbing away at the medical instruments she was sterilizing, knowing that whatever Dr. Dumont was about to propose would be another step in her journey from Hettie's daughter to her own kind of healer.

"What I hope to do is train you as a midwife," Dr. Dumont said. "The rates of maternal mortality in this community are far too high, and so much of it is preventable with adequate antenatal care and a skilled birth attendant. You have the intelligence and the instincts to do that kind of work, and you're trusted with the community in a way that they'd never trust in an outsider."

The responsibility of Dr. Dumont's proposal weighed on Carrie like a heavy cloak. Midwifery meant getting called out in the wee hours. It meant holding women's lives, and their babies' lives, in the balance—and becoming part of families' most intimate, precious moments.

But it also meant closing the circle that had started with watching Hettie take care of everyone on Saint Ann Street. It meant applying all her intelligence and compassion toward bringing new life safely into the world, supporting mothers through their most difficult times, and helping families grow strong and healthy.

"Yes," Carrie said without hesitation. "I wanna learn all that you can teach me."

The training would be hard; studying the stages of labor, for example, and learning to watch for complications that required prompt intervention or even practicing how to handle difficult deliveries. But the new role would take more than technical skills. It required an ever-present capacity for deep compassion that Carrie had spent most of her life developing—a capacity that began growing in Hettie's house.

On her way home to Saint Ann Street that evening, Carrie was filled with the same rightness she had when she first started nursing. This was her purpose: to heal not only the sick, but also to support health; not only to respond to crises, but to promote prevention; not only to care for individuals, but to strengthen the whole community by making sure those about to join it were brought carefully into this life.

She would soon be the person families called when new life was ready to enter the world. At all hours, she would walk through Selma's neighborhoods armed with her medical bag and healing hands, carrying on the tradition of service she had learned from Hettie, but now possessed with the power to save lives that might otherwise be lost.

The midwifery education course started that fall, as the Alabama River ran low and the cotton fields around Selma promised to whiten against the darkening earth. Dr. Dumont had positioned Carrie to work under experienced midwives in Birmingham and Montgomery, where she was learning things that could not be taught from a book.

"Birth is the most natural thing in the world, and also the most dangerous," Mrs. Sarah Johnson, a midwife who had been delivering babies for twenty-five years, told Carrie. "Every woman's body knows what to do, but sometimes you have to help it remember, and sometimes you need to know when to get help fast."

Carrie took it all in: how to keep track of the progress of labor, how to position women so they felt comfortable, how to know whether signs were pointing toward a birthing process where a baby would be in danger or bleeding was heading toward being too much. She learned to trust her hands as well as her eyes, feeling for the baby's position, checking for dilation of the cervix, and recognizing by touch what was happening inside a woman's body.

But mastering technical skills was only part of what she had to do. Midwifery was helping mothers discover courage they didn't know they had, while being a source of quiet strength during women's most vulnerable hours and supporting families through the sacred mystery of birth.

"The most important thing you have in your bag," Mrs. Johnson told her, "is who you are. Women in labor want to know that there is someone with them who gets what's happening, not somebody who will panic if things start getting intense."

By Christmas time in 1945, Carrie finally felt confident enough to attend a birth on her own, but Dr. Dumont remained available for questions and emergencies. Her first single-handed call was on Mrs. Ruth Coleman, a young mother whose husband was employed in the lumber mill and who resided in a small house three blocks from Saint Ann Street.

The call arrived at two o'clock in the morning on a cold January morning. Carrie put on an outfit, grabbed her medical bag, and walked the silent streets of Selma toward where Mrs. Coleman stood with her mother and mother-in-law, just three women trying to handle the intensifying contractions that indicated the baby would be coming soon.

"How you feeling, Mrs. Coleman?" Carrie inquired as she ushered the women back into the house, washed her hands, and checked on her patient.

"Scared," came the honest answer. "This is my first baby, and I can't help but think about all the things that could go wrong."

"That's normal," Carrie said, checking the baby's position. "But, so far, everything's fine. Your baby is in the proper position, and your body is doing what it's supposed to do. We're in this together."

For the next four hours, Carrie coached Mrs. Coleman through labor as she kept both mother and baby safe, encouraging the woman, comforting her through the pain, and working on details that made the difference between a safe delivery and a dangerous one. When the baby finally came—a rosy-cheeked boy who let out loud cries to announce his arrival—Carrie again experienced that deep satisfaction she'd known the moment she first discovered nursing was her calling.

But this was deeper still. She hadn't just been helping to cure someone who was sick; she'd helped deliver a baby into the world safely, accompanied a woman through one of the most difficult experiences she would ever endure, and ensured that a family's happiness wouldn't be tinged with tragedy.

News of Carrie's competence as a midwife circulated through Selma's colored community just as rapidly and efficiently as the word spread that she was capable of doing what the clinic did by herself in people's homes. Before long, she started getting calls two or three times a week, sometimes planned visits for women approaching their due dates, sometimes urgent summons in the middle of the night when labor unexpectedly took hold.

The work was physically demanding and emotionally intense. Carrie would walk miles through Selma's neighborhoods, carrying her medical bag and the portable equipment she needed for deliveries. She learned to navigate by moonlight, to locate homes in neighborhoods she had never before seen, to work by lamplight when electricity wasn't available.

Each birth was unique; each woman carried her own fears and strengths into the process. Some were fast and simple; others took hours of patient handholding, including careful observation. Carrie acquired the ability to recognize the subtle signs that distinguished normal changes from true troubles, and she learned to gauge when a problem warranted Dr. Dumont's immediate attention.

"You're getting quite a reputation," Dr. Dumont told Carrie one morning, looking over from the week's deliveries. "Mrs. Patterson came by yesterday to tell me that through you, her daughter's life had been saved during that complicated birth last month."

Mrs. Patterson's birth had been a tough one, a breech that had required delicate twisting to avoid complications. But Carrie stayed calm, followed the instruction she'd received, and helped safely deliver a healthy baby girl when things could have taken a swift, tragic turn.

"I only did what you taught me to do," Carrie responded.

"No, you did more than that. You applied your judgment, intuition, and capacity to keep it all together in the face of tension. Those aren't things you can teach. They're gifts that you brought to this work."

By the spring of 1946, Carrie's days had become filled with her duties at the clinic and also her rising midwifing work. She worked mornings at the clinic on Broad Street, serving patients with Dr. Dumont, and spent some afternoons and evenings visiting pregnant women in their homes or responding to calls for deliveries.

The work was already shaping her in ways she was still only beginning to realize. Every delivery she made bolstered her confidence; every family she assisted pulled her further into the community's web of relationships and trust. She was evolving into someone people came to for not only medical care, but also for the kind of reassuring, compassionate presence that helps a family get through life's most significant moments.

At the same time, Carrie was steadily growing more curious about having a family of her own. Her prospective husband Clarence Jones had been walking her home from the clinic more often than not. He would wait for her outside the clinic when she worked late, holding her medical bag as they walked through Selma's evening streets, listening as she talked over the day's challenges and victories. They would converse about books he was reading and dreams they both secretly kept of where their futures might take them. The concept of marriage had begun to seem less like something in the distant future and more like a natural next step in a life that was falling out precisely as it should.

But in the meantime, there was more to learn, more families to serve, and more skills to master. The stage was being set for everything that would come next for Carrie: the years at 1421 Sylvan Street, the nine children who would call her Mommie, all those nights spent helping women birth babies safely, and somehow finding time to raise her own children with the conviction that service to others is life's highest calling.

The man whom Carrie would marry, Clarence Jones, known to his family as "Red," was born in 1926 in Brantley, Alabama. Official documents would later mark his birth year as 1925 because that's what he told records keepers in the military when he was old enough to serve. When World War II broke out, he fibbed about his birth year to satisfy the enlistment age of eighteen. He considered it his duty to put his life on the line for his country, and he would not let his age hold him back.

During the war years, Clarence was an ammunitions truck driver in Europe with the United States Army—dangerous, but essential work that kept supply lines moving while fighting raged all around. Trucks like his contained the explosives that American military forces needed to defeat fascism. One mistake, one enemy shell finding its mark, and his life would have ended in a fireball exploding on some European road or field he might not even have known the name of. But Clarence made it through the war and returned home in 1946.

Like many Black veterans arriving home from Europe, Clarence returned a different man. He had proudly donned his country's uniform. He had served among men of different races. He had seen places where Jim Crow's suffocating grip wasn't so tight. He had put his life at risk for principles of freedom and democracy that his own country denied him in his own home.

He came back to Alabama hoping for, if not equality, at least a little acknowledgment that he'd proven himself a full citizen. He'd fought against fascism in pursuit of freedom abroad. Surely that meant something.

Instead, what he found was the same Selma he'd left: a city where Black residents still couldn't vote, couldn't eat at downtown lunch counters, couldn't drink from water fountains frequented by white people, and couldn't access equal education or employment or justice. The contradiction must have burned his chest every time he walked downtown, every time he was forced to step aside in white people's presence, every time he saw signs that designated COLORED and WHITE as distinct—and decisively unequal—facilities.

He'd driven trucks through war-ravaged Europe. He'd faced enemy fire. He was a veteran of a nation that had pledged liberty and justice for all. And yet he couldn't cast a ballot in Dallas County.

The experience Clarence and countless other Black veterans had of fighting for freedom overseas that they were denied at home would be one of the crucibles in which the modern civil rights movement was forged. These were men who had seen too much, risked too much, to endure second-class citizenship with a silent smile. Their service had changed them, and they were going to change America.

But none of that came before Carrie Lundy.

The courtship between Carrie and Clarence Jones began when the two were introduced by Clarence's youngest sister Essie, a student at Knox Academy where Carrie also attended. Essie was a grade behind Carrie and felt that her brother and her friend would be cute together—and that both were ready for something more than what Selma seemed to offer a young Black couple in those years. As with most things of consequence in their community, the romance between Carrie and Clarence Jones developed effortlessly. Over shared strolls after Carrie finished her clinic shifts, and talks on Hettie's front porch, the two would eventually learn that they both balanced each other in ways that boded well for a solid partnership.

Carrie had known quite a number of young men who were at least as interesting as Clarence. But, where others may have been put off by Carrie's professional obligations and the demands of her calling, Clarence seemed to recognize that her work was part of who she was, not something that would go away after she married.

"You think differently than other people," he said to her one night as they sat on the steps of Green Street Baptist Church, watching the sun drop behind the Alabama River. "You look at problems and solve them. You see the hurting that people are facing and how you can help them heal."

"Mama always told me we're here for people," Carrie said. "The nursing and midwifery taught me better tools for doing what I was raised to do."

"That's what I mean. The general belief is that work is what you do to make money. To you, work is what you *have* to do."

Even better, Clarence just seemed to fit in perfectly with Carrie's extended family, which made their courtship even more precious. Carrie's brothers, Willie, Isaac, and John accepted him right off. They loved his intelligence and his true concern for their lives.

Willie, who was pursuing his own professional aspirations, discovered in Clarence a kindred spirit when it came to reading and learning. They would spend evenings on Hettie's front porch debating anything from politics to philosophy, as Clarence helped both Willie and Isaac work through the personal challenges they were wrestling with.

More practically, John appreciated Clarence's readiness to help with whatever needed doing. Years after Carrie and Clarence were married, John eventually constructed a grand barbecue pit in his sister's backyard. Several men from the family joined in the work, like Carrie's younger brother Sylvester "DeeDee" Lundy, a fun-loving painter and brick mason who always played and laughed with all the children in the extended family. Clarence was right there with the men, mixing concrete and placing bricks. His bookishness did not preclude him from using his hands when help was called for.

"He's good people," John said to Carrie after one of these working sessions. "Intelligent but not an intellectual-showoff type thing. And he sees what you do with your work—really sees you, and respects that."

It was this family life that Clarence Jones, armed with a practiced ask and an acute sense of urgency, was requesting to share when he proposed to Carrie early in 1946. On July 22, as soon as Carrie graduated from high school, the two eloped. Carrie was nineteen years old, Clarence twenty-one. They took their vows with the same determination and independence that had drawn them together.

After the ceremoniless elopement, Clarence took Carrie back to her home at 1410 Saint Ann Street, and then returned to his own family's home in Brantley. As the story goes, when he told his father what he had done, his father told him, "You get back to Selma right now, go to Carrie's house, and tell her mother what you did."

So Clarence went back and faced Hettie, informing her that he'd married her daughter without seeking permission, without the traditional courtship, and without even allowing the families enough time to prepare.

That return trip—the young veteran going back to face the consequences of his impulsive decision—says something essential about both Clarence and the values his father instilled in him. You could be bold, but you had to answer for yourself. You could go where your heart led, but you had to confront the people whom your choices affected. You could be self-reliant, but you could not evade duty.

For her part, Hettie must have appraised this young veteran who had spirited away her daughter. Hettie would have seen a man who had served his country, who'd followed his father's advice to come face his new mother-in-law, who loved Carrie enough that he moved quickly but was also responsible enough to make things right.

Whatever she thought, Carrie and Clarence began their married life together: a World War II veteran who'd risked his life for a country that still denied him basic rights, and a young woman who would prove just as courageous in different ways.

The elopement was just another example of the kind of practical people they were. They didn't need lavish ceremonies to express their commitment to one another and to the work that both felt called on earth to accomplish. Their shared value was to do something that mattered to them, together.

Several months later, as Carrie was preparing to leave the clinic one evening, Dr. Dumont approached her with an unusually serious expression.

"Carrie, can I talk to you for a few minutes before you head out? I have something important that I need to discuss with you." The doctor nodded towards the chairs in her private office.

When they sat, Dr. Dumont leaned in with the intense engagement she brought to her most important decisions. "I've been watching you these last few years. You're my nurse no more—you are truly my partner. The community believes in everything you do, and your talent has evolved so much more than even I predicted."

Carrie leaned in, feeling like something big was about to be said.

"I'd like to help you and Clarence buy a house," Dr. Dumont said. "A home to have your family while we continue working together. There's a house on Sylvan Street that would be perfect; big enough for the family you'll want to have, centrally located for your midwifery calls, and affordable with the proper financial arrangement."

The terms were more than Carrie had dared to hope for, but she knew they came with obligations and commitments beyond mere lending.

"I can put in the down payment and help to create good terms for monthly payments, if I am able," Dr. Dumont continued. "I would want your promise of continuing to work with me for at least the next five years, and your commitment to provide a home that we could use as an informal adjunct to our medical care when necessary."

It was a partnership that would benefit everyone involved. Dr. Dumont would have a skilled, committed colleague; the community would have continued access to quality medical care; and Carrie and Clarence would have the foundation they needed to build their own family while continuing to serve others.

"We'll be good stewards of the house," Carrie said, "and we'll fulfill that promise we're making around the work. I'm sure Clarence will be just as grateful for this opportunity as I am."

"I know you will. That's why I'm offering this opportunity."

It wasn't before long that Carrie and Clarence settled into 1421 Sylvan Street—a small, seven-room home which would eventually become the hub around which their village of supporters and caregivers formed. The house came with a big yard that could accommodate children's play and socializing, rooms to act as makeshift examining spaces when medical needs presented themselves, and a kitchen that would prepare healthful food for scores of neighbors and family members in the decades ahead.

The couple's first neighbors said that 1421 Sylvan Street was situated at the center of a very giving community. In the house to the right lived Mrs. Tena Smith, a widow, and Ms. Emma McCracken. The two were washwomen who did white folks' laundry, and Carrie could see their table of work from her own back yard—the big black iron pot sitting on a fire log, clothes being stirred and swirled around in boiling water with Octagon flakes.

These women became priceless to Carrie in her budding medical practice. They knew that Dr. Dumont's clinical duties and midwifery calls might come at any hour, and they were ever willing to assist with Carrie's home and family when medical emergencies demanded Carrie's immediate aid.

Dr. Dumont had chosen well. The house was well placed for Carrie's growing role as the community's midwife and first point of medical contact. It was close enough to the clinic for consultation, it was conveniently centered among her serving families, and large enough to house the children that were soon to arrive.

The first of those children, Gwendolyn, was born in 1947, and Carrie discovered that being a mother only deepened her understanding of what other women experienced during pregnancy and childbirth. Now she knew firsthand the fears and joys of waiting for a baby, the bodily difficulties of carrying one, and the weighty sense of responsibility that washed over her when she held her own in her arms.

"Motherhood makes you a better midwife," she said to Dr. Dumont one morning as she was about to leave the clinic for a delivery. Baby Gwendolyn was sleeping peacefully in a basket next to the examination table. "When you have been there yourself, you become aware of what women want in ways that would have simply never occurred to you."

The routine of life at 1421 Sylvan Street began to take hold: clinical work during the day, midwifery calls at all hours and, in between, the daily chores of raising her own children and managing a home that doubled as an informal clinic for anyone who needed care.

It was an all-consuming life, but it was also deeply rewarding. Each successful delivery increased her reputation and bolstered her confidence. Every family she assisted drew her deeper into the community's web of relationships. Each child she delivered safely added to the growing strength and health of the neighborhood that was her own.

And more and more people were starting to refer to the children who played in her big yard and walked to school together as "Carrie's kids," an acknowledgment that 1421 Sylvan Street was no longer just a house, but a hub of family, of communal life for all who came on its path.

CHAPTER THREE

Carrie's House on Sylvan Street

I thank God for my ten children. I also pray for them at this time. Thank you, Lord, for always being there for me.
—Carrie Louise, Sept. 20, 1998

The house at 1421 Sylvan Street appeared modest from the road, but to Carrie and Clarence it represented the future of everything they'd dreamed of building together. Seven rooms of possibility, surrounded by a large rectangular yard that offered ample space for the children they planned to have and the community that would naturally gather around Carrie's work.

Like a framed picture, 1421 Sylvan Street was bordered on all sides by a chain-link fence. The fence served not as a barrier, but as a gentle boundary defining the space where their family would grow and their service to the community would thrive. Along the front left and right sides, pink running roses climbed the fence, blooming most of the year as they filled the air with their sweet fragrance. A tall pecan tree, planted years ago by Mrs. Tena Smith, the woman who'd be their first neighbor, stood in the front right corner of the fence. The tree would eventually provide a shady spot and a quiet refuge for children who needed a moment away from rough play or the bustle of family life.

The house itself was typical of Selma homes built for working families in the 1940s and 50s—a single-story wooden frame with wood siding, raised on brick platform pillars that lifted it thirty inches off the ground to protect against river flooding. At the front of the house, the living room faced the street. Behind the living room was a dining room and the adjacent kitchen that would become the heart of family life. Three bedrooms occupied the right side of the house, with a bathroom and back porch attached to the rear where the family washed clothes.

Yet it would be the yard that defined life at 1421 Sylvan Street. To the right side, between the house and the fence, lay a walkway and a space just big enough for a children's garden that would produce tomatoes, cucumbers, and yellow squash each summer. To the left side, another pecan tree shaded a wider space between fence and house, a relatively cool play area where children could hide from the Alabama summer's heat. The wide backyard extended to the alley, where a third pecan tree bordered the neighbors on the street behind them.

This earthy yard, which Carrie's future sons would constantly rake and clear as they became old enough for chores, would eventually hold a few items precious to family life: the famous basketball goal that reached twelve feet high, Uncle John's impressive barbecue pit with its beautifully designed chimney stack, and the in-ground duck pond that would accommodate the growing flock that began with two ducks from Ms. Elvira.

"This is going to be perfect," Carrie said to Clarence as they paced through the empty house on moving day, with baby Gwendolyn asleep in her arms. "Lots of room for our little ones to play, not too far from the clinic so I can get there in a hurry, and big enough to accommodate whatever medical situations may come to us."

Clarence nodded, already imagining where his books would go, how a dining room table could pull double duty for homework and family meetings, the corner where he could carve out a spot for the reading and thinking that helped to sustain him. But he also knew that his home would never be solely a private space. 1421 Sylvan Street would be a community resource, where neighbors turned for help and children played and families sought support in their difficult times.

Mrs. Tena and Ms. Emma were ideal first neighbors for a young family. They knew what it was like to have full-time work away from home during the day and full-time work at home with young children, and they eagerly jumped in when Carrie was needed at deliveries or for emergencies.

"Go on and see to whoever you have to," Mrs. Tena would say when Carrie would abruptly leave for a midwife call. "We'll be sure to keep an eye on things here and feed Clarence if you're away past supper time."

They would be the first to join the long list of neighbors who supportively babysat both baby Gwendolyn and, later, her younger siblings. The network of mutual assistance that would hold the family together for decades was already in place. Within walking distance were at least five Black-owned corner stores and cafés where Carrie's family was known and loved: Mr. Mason's Deli and Groceries, Mr. and Mrs. Losker Smith's Café, Mrs. Alberta's Café, Danzy's Café and Gaines Grocery. This neighborly support represented a village that made it possible for Carrie to serve families throughout Selma while she raised her own.

Life at 1421 Sylvan Street settled into a routine in short order. In the mornings, Carrie headed out, usually down to the clinic on Broad Street, sometimes walking, some mornings accepting a ride from Ms. Joan in her MG convertible. Her days were full of patients who needed care and expectant mothers who needed monitoring, and she continuously took part in training that kept her skills sharp and current.

But it was the evenings and nights that showed what they were really building. Word traveled through the neighborhood that Carrie and Clarence were making their home on Sylvan Street, and people started showing up at their door at hours the clinic was unavailable or with problems that the clinic was not equipped to solve.

What the house became would not have been possible without the man who planted its seeds as a family home. Clarence Jones Sr.*

was born in 1926 to Henry and Edna Jones, the youngest of their five children in a sharecropper family that farmed on the other side of the river from Selma, in Brantley, Alabama. The love between Clarence and Carrie would be the start of everything that would follow at 1421 Sylvan Street.

Clarence Sr., whom the children lovingly called "Daddy," was bookish and kindly, a man who possessed no college degrees but who read more books than did most degree holders. If asked whether he ever attended college, he'd deny it with a chuckle and say, "I went in the front door and came out the back." Though he was as unpretentious a man as you could meet, he couldn't hide his intelligence or how important reading had been to shaping his view of things.

He was always well turned out but never ostentatious, and he carried himself with a certain quiet dignity that caused people to stop for a second look. In his own way, he was striking, with a strong jaw and a way of speaking that made you sit up straighter when he spoke. Some of his neighbors would've added that he was as handsome as Clark Gable, not just in appearance, but in his charisma, charm, and what they perceived as an unexpectedly soft-edged tenderness. The neighborhood kids adored him.

Around the neighborhood, Clarence Sr. was known as a defender of those who needed defending. One day a message came home about him, saying that he had interfered when a man was being bullied. Words were exchanged and fists thrown, and he came back with a fractured jaw but a peaceful heart. When asked why he had intervened, he had shrugged and replied, "Some things are worth fighting for, even if it doesn't look like the odds are in your favor."

Clarence Sr. stacked all sorts of books in the living room bookcase: history, biography, philosophy, novels, even a French-language version of Les Misérables. In the evenings after work, the man could often be found reading there and occasionally relating what he'd read to whoever wanted to listen. When Gwendolyn pondered ideals like fairness and justice, often sparked by the unfair treatment of people in their Black

---

* From this point forward, I will refer to my father by the full name Clarence Jones Sr.

neighborhood, Daddy was the one to fan his daughter's imagination. Not through lofty orations but by showing that thinking aloud was natural and that books were doorways to power. She would later attribute her career in law in part to his influence, recognizing how he had sown seeds that grew throughout her life.

Though not trained or skilled in medicine, Clarence was a true partner in his wife's medical work. One night Mrs. Williams, who lived down the street, showed up with her younger son, who'd gashed his hand in play and required stitches that couldn't wait till the morning clinic opened. Carrie washed and bandaged the injury by lamplight at her kitchen table as Clarence amused the boy with tales to soothe him.

Every few weeks or so, Clarence Sr. would load some or all of the children into whatever vehicle they had and take them to visit his parents and extended family in Brantley, Alabama. These trips to what most folks in Selma called "the country" weren't just family obligations. To us children, they were journeys to a different time and place. It was a world our father knew; it helped us understand where we had come from and appreciate what they had on Sylvan Street.

Uncle William, Clarence Sr.'s eldest brother, was a sharecropper who cultivated every kind of vegetable: corn and beans, peanuts and peach trees, sugar cane and watermelons. The children loved these visits, experiencing farm life and animals, playing with our six cousins who lived only five minutes' drive down the road from our grandparents' house. While the country cousins loved to have us visit, they teased that when the Selma children came, we would eat up all their food.

The farmhouses were small and built entirely of wood, with that weathered gray appearance typical of buildings that had withstood many seasons. The porches sagged beneath the weight of talkers, and water came from wells and hand pumps. Their aunt and grandmother both did their cooking on cast-iron wood-fired stoves. The Selma children would marvel at the entire meals that came out of that primitive yet remarkably efficient way of cooking.

The visits were valuable learning experiences for the children about family and resourcefulness and the dignity of agricultural work. We learned that prosperity was not about having modern comforts, but having more than enough food to share, close-knit family relations, satisfaction from working hard, and providing for our own. The differences between life in the city and life in the country helped the children value both places and recognize that there are many ways of living meaningfully.

The coming of Carrie and Clarence Sr.'s second child, Carolyn, in 1949, and then Yolanda in 1950 and Joan in 1951, truly made 1421 Sylvan Street into a home. With four children all under the age of four, Carrie had to put systems and schedules in place that would help her do professional work when motherhood was pulling at her from every direction.

This is when the household demonstrated its true genius as a focal point of community life and its design served its anticipated purposes. That large dining room fed the growing family, and anyone else who came to the door needing to be fed. The kitchen served as a center of activity where Carrie would cook and keep an eye on the kids as well as whatever medical concern was developing in the living room.

The front porch turned into an informal waiting area where a neighbor could discuss health problems or concerns with Carrie without scheduling appointments at the clinic. The backyard was a safe place for children to play under the watchful eyes of the numerous adults who understood that raising children was the work of community.

"You can't do it by yourself," Mrs. Tena said quietly one afternoon as she helped Carrie hang laundry while four children flocked around them. "No woman can work the way you work and have babies like you're having without help."

"I'm not doing this by myself," Carrie replied, gesturing toward the network of support around them. "Just look at how things are: I have you and Ms. Emma watching out, Mrs. Coleman when she makes too much food to bring a part over, Mr. Parnell fixing plumbing if anything is leaking or gets broken, and Clarence running everything at home whenever the phone rings for me."

This was the groundwork from which all else would follow: the twins Frederick and Clarence Jr., born in 1953, Carrie's growing midwifery practice, the civil rights work that would turn their children into local activists, and all those countless nights when families in need would arrive at their door and know they could get help.

When the first pair of twins came along, the household gained new vitality and a need for additional discipline. With six children under the age of six, Carrie would need to become an expert in efficiency and delegation. The older girls, Gwendolyn and Carolyn, pitched in, mastering diaper changing and bottle feeding and any number of other details that made sure the babies were comfortable and safe.

The physical place of 1421 Sylvan Street was beginning to look like what Dr. Dumont dreamed it would be when she helped Carrie and Clarence Sr. buy it: not just a home for the family, but a community hub where medical care, childcare, spiritual support, and practical help came together naturally. Where kids learned by seeing that service to others was life's highest calling. Where neighbors understood that everyone's wellbeing depended on everyone's willingness to help each other.

The streets of Selma, and especially Sylvan Street, were more than just thoroughfares between one place and another. They were the primary playground where children spent countless hours in games, exploration, and the kind of unstructured play that built both character and community bonds. Streets and sidewalks in this area were not like those found in white neighborhoods. Both the sidewalks and streets in the Black sections of town were mixtures of sand and clay, creating surfaces that were perfectly suited for the activities of children that fill their days from sun-up until bedtime.

All the neighborhood kids played football, softball (which the kids called stickball), and kickball right on the streets under the watchful gaze of neighbors who understood that protecting their community was something they all did. The kids had no structure or adult management; we met up and played when we were done with doing what needed to be done around the house, and we kept playing until it was time to go home for supper or the streetlights came on.

But at 1421 Sylvan Street, there was one rule to rule them all when it came to playtime: There was no play until we did the work. Carrie's offspring knew that while our chores and studying for school took top priority over fun, once we did what was expected of us, we could participate in the neighborhood games that brought life to Sylvan Street with the sounds of happy children.

The sand and clay streets created their own seasonal rhythms that became part of the natural cycle of Sylvan Street life. When the roads were muddied after days of heavy rain, the city would eventually send a tractor with a scraper blade to restore the surfaces, an event that fascinated the children who would watch the heavy machinery transform our temporary obstacle course back into a proper playing field.

But more memorable than the practical restoration of the playing field was the sensory experience that always followed the rain. The sweet smell of the earth after a storm, that distinctive aroma of wet clay and sand mixed with the green scents of growing things, would fill the air and create the kind of olfactory memory that would last lifetimes. Years later, the smell would take us right back to our childhood in Selma, evoking for us summer afternoons when the heaviest decision was whether to play dodgeball or set up a game of hide and seek.

The lessons learned during the street games could not be taught in any classroom. Children learned how to work out rules, include younger players without ruining the game, settle disputes fairly, and realize that individual skill was pointless in a vacuum if someone else didn't cooperate and make getting games off the ground possible. They learned physical coordination, strategic thinking, and the type of social intelligence that would aid them over their lives.

The evening was when the house truly showed its character. Once supper dishes were cleared, homework splayed out across the dining room table, you might hear the telltale hum and clatter of Carrie's Singer foot-pedal sewing machine. Sometimes the machine whirred after the younger children had gone to bed at night, sometimes on a Saturday afternoon, sometimes even before dawn if there was something she needed to complete before the day's responsibilities began demanding her time.

The sewing machine sat in a corner that became Carrie's home base for clothing production. She made dresses for all four girls, often using fabrics as far as they would go and creating matching outfits that announced these children belonged together. Any scraps that remained would be transformed into something useful—potholders, doll clothes, patches for worn knees. Nothing was wasted when so many children needed to be clothed and resources were limited.

Her pattern-cutting station was the dining room table. She would drape fabric over its length, then carefully pin pattern pieces to it with straight pins before cutting out what, to the children, appeared to be puzzle pieces that magically became school uniforms and church dresses or the matching cotton jackets and short pants she especially loved making for me and my twin brother Frederick during summer months.

When the girls had to leave for boarding school, she would sit in her room stitching their names into every item of clothing, a laborious task that ensured nothing would be permanently lost in big loads of wash. The curtains that hung in every window were her creation, remade each spring when the house needed refreshing. Even some of the family's church clothes were sewn by her practiced hands and her resolve that her children would be well-dressed regardless of their economic circumstances.

It wasn't just about clothing the family; it was dignity and presentation. Carrie realized that her children's appearance when they walked through Selma influenced their reception and their self-image. Well-sewn clothes, well-pressed uniforms, and Sunday dresses that looked like they came from a store—even when they hadn't. That was how she prevented economic limitations from sliding into social diminishment.

But beyond the practical necessity, the sewing sessions taught lessons about patience, precision, and the changing of raw materials into finished products through careful attention and skilled work. The children watched their mother take flat pieces of fabric and create three-dimensional clothing that fit properly and looked professional. They learned that quality work required time, that shortcuts produced inferior results, and that taking pride in what you created was as important as the creation itself.

During these sewing sessions, the radio or record player would be playing the music Carrie loved: Mahalia Jackson's powerful gospel, Dinah Washington's smooth jazz, Sam Cooke's soul, Aretha Franklin's commanding voice, the sophisticated phrasing of Sarah Vaughan and Nat King Cole, even Patsy Cline's country heartbreak and Etta James's blues. This was Mommie's music, the soundtrack of her evening work, and the children absorbed it along with their spelling words and arithmetic problems.

"Y'all doing your homework?" she would inquire without raising her head from her sewing, her foot maintaining its steady rhythm on the pedal.

"Yes ma'am," the chorus of replies would come from children spread around the dining room table with books, papers, and multiplication tables.

Sometimes she would hum along with whatever was playing, her voice blending with Mahalia's or matching Dinah's phrasing, creating a domestic symphony that made even difficult homework feel manageable—the sewing machine's rhythmic humming, the music's emotional depth, and occasionally Carrie's own voice blending with the professionals on the record player.

These were the hours when the house felt most like home, because daytime problems surrendered to quieter activities that bonded the family in its proximity and its mission. Older kids would help younger kids read or do math, and we all understood that helping the younger ones extended as much to homework as it did to chores.

On Saturdays, the music would change. Casey Kasem's American Top 40 would fill the house with the popular songs that the children loved, creating a different kind of soundtrack for weekend chores and activities. This was their music, the hits they heard at Ben's Barbecue Cafe, the songs that defined their generation. But it was Carrie who made space for it in their home, realizing that children needed their own cultural connection even as she was teaching them to appreciate the deeper traditions she valued.

The house itself had to accommodate the growing family's needs. An expansion of the boys' room would now support four bunk beds, and a bedroom added to the back of the house provided space for Rubie, a student from Good Samaritan's nursing program who became like an older sister to the children. Gwen, prior to leaving home for college, would share a room with Rubie. Rubie's presence provided additional supervision when Carrie was away for deliveries, and her nursing training meant she could manage any minor medical situations that arose.

Most importantly, however, Sherman would enter the world during a period of transformation for Selma that would adjust not just the trajectory of the Jones family's lives but also their community. The civil rights movement was boiling up all over the South, and Selma was too central a place to not be noticed by activists who understood its strategic potential.

"Things are changing," Dr. Dumont said one day, as she and Carrie sat in the living room at 1421 Sylvan Street and discussed the growing hostility they felt in their community. "I'm getting questions on voter registration drives and on organizing efforts. I think we're probably going to see some pretty seismic, transformative sort of shifts here in the next couple years."

Carrie nodded, thinking of her own kids and wondering what this could all mean for them. The older ones had already displayed enough intelligence and courage to convince her that they would not be content to live under the status quo of segregation. They grew up in a home where their mother made service to others her life's work; they saw how standing for what is right and just is far more important than mere self-interest.

"My kids are going to be prepared for whatever comes," Carrie said. "They're learning how to think for themselves, they're learning how to care about other people, and they believe that they make a difference in the world."

This confidence would prove prophetic. Then, with the arrival of the second pair of twins Christopher and Anthony in 1959, pushing the number of children to nine, the house at 1421 Sylvan Street was more than a large family's home: It was becoming a kind of launchpad for a new generation of civil rights activists.

The second twins' birth complicated things further, yet it deepened the structure that they'd laid down together as a family for more than ten years. Everybody knew what it was that they were supposed to do, and everybody knew that their family was not like other families, nor was their mother's work like other mothers' work—and that was okay.

"We're not the same as other families," Carrie told her children during one of their regular Family Meeting get-togethers, as they sat around the dining room table. "We have more children than most families, more things to worry about than most families, and we simply have more opportunities for change. That also means working harder and loving each other more and knowing that what we do is for all of us."

We children understood. We'd seen our mother attend births around the clock, nurse anyone who needed medical help, and care for everyone in the household, which also happened to serve as something of an informal community center. We knew success wasn't just your own getting ahead; it also meant that other people could rely on you.

These lessons in service and accountability would serve us well in the trials ahead. By 1960, with nine children, ranging from newborn twins to thirteen-year-old Gwendolyn, the house at 1421 Sylvan Street was ready to play its role in the movement that would change American history.

The Jones family had built the edifice: close personal connections to family, deep community roots, and a wealth of instances of helping others, with children who knew they were being raised for lives that mattered. They would be ready for whatever came next.

CHAPTER FOUR

The Impossible Distance

Clarence Sr. relished the role he played in aiding Carrie's calling, but he never envisioned himself solely as a support to the medical mission. As a husband and father, he wanted to provide for his family financially. Yet finding steady, decent-paying work was one of his most difficult challenges during the 1950s. Like so many other Black men in Selma during the Jim Crow period, he learned that intelligence, determination, and work ethic couldn't always overcome the economic limitations that segregation imposed on Black families.

For a while, he sold insurance policies in the Black community for the Booker T. Washington Life Insurance Company and later the Atlanta Life Insurance Company, offering financial products and services that mainstream companies didn't always make available to Black families. It was honorable work and met a critical community need, but the pay was intermittent, relying heavily on commissions from sales that could vary from month to month.

He also drove a few hours a week for the Southwind Cab Company, owned by a friend of his, ferrying people around the Black community in Selma. Again, the work was honest and necessary, but the economic rewards were stifled by a segregated economy that limited where he could pick up passengers and what fares he could charge.

Racial prejudice was palpable in Clarence Sr.'s working life. One rainy day, before he started taxiing passengers all around Selma, he dropped some of his children off to school in his taxicab. As the children were exiting the vehicle, a white police officer shouted gruffly at Clarence Sr., "Boy, move that vehicle on!"

Keeping his emotions in check, Clarence Sr. responded, "Yes, sir, officer—just as soon as I let the boys out for school." He hurried the boys along under the officer's annoyed gaze.

His eldest daughter Gwendolyn was in the car with him and witnessed the whole encounter. When he got back in the car, she asked him, "Daddy, why did the policeman call you a boy? You are a man!"

Over time, Clarence Sr. grew frustrated at not being able to support his expanding family in a manner that matched his abilities on top of being disrespected and discriminated against in the working world. Irritation and annoyance at not finding proper work began to wear on Clarence Sr.'s nerves and disposition in ways not immediately apparent to the children but increasingly noticeable to Carrie. He spent his evenings reading help-wanted advertisements in newspapers from Cleveland, Detroit, and other cities north of the Mason-Dixon line whose economies had already been adapting to the demands of a modern society—cities where he might find an opportunity that would allow him to use his capabilities as fully as any man might be permitted.

The Great Migration was carrying many men in Selma to northern cities with better jobs, higher wages, and greater opportunities for advancement. Clarence Sr.'s Uncle Sherman was already in Cleveland and had written back about work that paid well enough to support a family decently, overtime opportunities, and chances for promotion simply not available to Black men in Alabama. Not long after Joan's birth, he decided to go find work in Cleveland, but he knew he would not be able to bring his young family with him at the start.

Much of what Clarence Sr. had heard about the job market in

northern cities turned out to be true: He was able to move into an apartment in a building that Uncle Sherman managed, find well-paying work, and send checks home to Selma on a regular basis. Yet the atmosphere was far from glamorous. He would often write home about how lonely he was. When Carrie left her four daughters in the care of neighbors and visited Cleveland, her husband's cramped, substandard living conditions alarmed her. She could not envision raising her children in that kind of environment, no matter what job opportunities the city offered.

When the twins Clarence Jr. and Frederick were born, Clarence Sr. returned to Selma to be with his family and try—futilely for the most part—to find sustainable employment. He was overjoyed to have the sons he and Carrie had been trying for, but a familiar frustration arose within him at the low-paying, off-and-on jobs he was forced to work. After a few years, he felt pulled back to Cleveland.

Clarence Sr.'s leaving Selma a second time in 1957 marked a turning point in the life of 1421 Sylvan Street. What had been a two-parent household managing the complex demands of professional medical practice and child-rearing, once again became a single-mother household where every system had to be reimagined and strengthened.

Clarence Sr.'s decision to leave Selma in search of work had not been made suddenly, but it felt sudden to the children who were four, six, seven, eight, nine, and ten years old. They knew Daddy was going to Cleveland again to try to find better work so he could send money home, but they could not understand what his leaving would do to their day-to-day lives or for how long he would be away.

In the first few years of his absence, there was always much expectation and hope. He would come home for Christmas or Thanksgiving, bearing gifts and stories of life in Cleveland, reassuring everyone that the separation would not be for long and that things would soon be better for the whole family. Sherman was born in 1958, a year after Clarence Sr. left, creating a bitter dynamic of a son who would be familiar with his father only through these holiday visits, never through daily presence.

"Please Come Home for Christmas" became the song that told

the children's feelings during these years, expressing both their love for their father and their wish that the family could be whole again. The holidays became times of deep, often conflicting emotions: great joy when Daddy did come home, sadness when he left, and increasing uncertainty of when they would see him again.

As the years went on, visits became less frequent and then ceased altogether. The reasons were complicated: the challenge of traveling from Cleveland to Selma, the emotional toll of saying goodbye over and over, and the eventual realization that his temporary absence had become permanent. Hopes that the family could be reunited in Cleveland or Selma were gradually disappearing in ways none of us had anticipated or desired.

The effect on each child was unique but life changing. Joan, who had been very close to our father, suffered what she would later call depression and trauma from hearing about our parents' separation and divorce. That summer, while all the other siblings went for an extended stay with family members in Birmingham, she needed to be at home, in familiar surroundings, and with plenty of extra emotional support during what was a hard time for her.

For me as one of the first pair of twin boys, the loss created feelings of abandonment and confusion that would persist well into my college years. My twin brother Frederick and I both loved to ride on our father's knees and hear his tall tales, and we had little understanding of why economic circumstances had to disrupt families, why good men could not find decent work in their own town, and why children were compelled to grow up without daily access to their fathers' guidance and affection.

Each of the siblings bore their own burden of this trauma, in how they grieved and experienced the loss, in ways that would influence their relationships, and in their understanding of family responsibility. Some reacted by becoming more independent, others by seeking additional responsibility, and still others by needing extra emotional support during a time when their mother's attention was spread thin.

The grief from our father's absence influenced how we supported each other during later challenges. It would also instill in most of us a determination to create stability for our own children when they became adults. We learned that love alone wasn't always enough to hold families together, that from time to time external forces could rupture even the strongest of bonds, and that resiliency is an essential survival skill.

I didn't understand then what I understood now about the trap my father found himself in. As children, we held onto hope—Christmas after Christmas, visit after visit, promise after promise. We never stopped believing Daddy would come home, would make it work, would bring us all together again. Mommie never let us give up on him, and we didn't. Looking back now as an adult with an engineer's mind and a historian's understanding of Jim Crow's systematic cruelty, I can see what none of us could articulate then: Clarence Sr. wasn't failing us. The system was designed to make men like him disappear.

The equation was impossible to solve from the start.

If Daddy stayed in Selma, there was no stable work for a Black man, no matter that he'd served his country in World War II, no matter his capabilities or determination. Jim Crow had seen to it that the deliberate denial of employment wasn't accidental; it was policy. Without work, he couldn't provide for a family that would eventually include nine children.

But if he left for Cleveland—which he did, seeking the stability we desperately needed—he faced a different impossibility. Because what made our survival possible in Selma couldn't be replicated six hundred miles north.

In Selma, despite every oppression Jim Crow could devise, we had a reliable infrastructure: Mommie had stable work at Dr. Dumont's clinic, which provided nursing income we could count on. Our grandmother Hettie lived close enough to help. Our country relatives brought food annually. Neighbors like Mrs. Willie Mae Dawson provided childcare when Mommie worked. With financial assistance from Dr. Dumont, all nine of us attended Saint Elizabeth Catholic School, where the Sisters of Saint Joseph knew us by name and invested in our futures. Brown Chapel African Methodist Episcopal Church anchored us spiritually and practically. We knew the rules—Jim Crow's vicious rules, yes, but rules we learned to navigate. As children, we rarely felt the effects of racial oppression in an acute way because our community protected and provided for us.

Cleveland promised none of this.

There was no Dr. Dumont offering Mommie stable employment. No Hettie to help with nine children. No network of neighbors who'd known us since birth. No Catholic school already invested in our education. No church community that considered us family. And most critically, no guarantee that Daddy's work would remain stable enough to replace everything we'd lose.

Given that uncertainty, for Mommie to uproot nine children and relocate to Cleveland wasn't love—it was gambling with our survival. She couldn't do it. And Daddy, six hundred miles away, had to live with that reality every single day.

I imagine—and this is speculation built on pieces my siblings later shared, but it's informed speculation—what that distance did to my father. He faced economic shame: a World War II veteran, an ammunition truck driver who'd served his nation proudly, returned to a country that denied him the dignity of providing for his family. Then there was the daily arithmetic of it all: Every visit cost money the family needed for other things. Every phone call was a reminder of separation. Every missed Christmas promise—and there were years when the shopping money he'd promised didn't arrive before Christmas, which made the lyrics of certain Christmas carols bitterly memorable—became another confirmation that the dream was slipping away.

My sister Carolyn, who later spent time in Cleveland and then Detroit where Daddy's siblings lived, learned things we children hadn't known. Daddy had PTSD symptoms—not surprising for a combat veteran, but there was no treatment available, not even public acknowledgment that Black veterans carried psychological wounds from serving a country that oppressed them. He started gambling, perhaps trying to win enough to make reunion possible, perhaps just trying to manage the stress and loneliness. He drank. He made promises he couldn't keep.

The realizations must have been gradual and devastating: Bringing the family to Cleveland was becoming less realistic each month, not more. Cleveland had its own racism, its own problems, its own uncertainties. What we had in Selma—as oppressive as it was—represented a stability he couldn't promise to replace.

This was Jim Crow working exactly as designed.

The system wasn't just about water fountains and lunch counters. It was about systematically fracturing Black families. Deny employment in the South, force men to migrate for work, separate them from their support systems, create impossible choices, ensure that even loving, capable fathers couldn't fulfill their roles. Make them disappear. Break the community bonds. Induce shame. Make it look like personal failure when it was systemic destruction.

Thousands of Black families experienced this same story during the Great Migration. It wasn't just opportunity-seeking northward movement—it was families torn apart by economic desperation, fathers who left intending to return but couldn't, mothers holding everything together in impossible circumstances, children growing up with absent fathers they remembered as loving.

As children, we didn't understand the systemic forces. We just knew we missed Daddy. We knew Mommie was managing alone. We knew the promises didn't always materialize. We knew the visits became less frequent, then stopped.

But here's what Mommie ensured, and what made all the difference in how we survived it: We never stopped hoping. We never gave up on our father. We didn't grow bitter or hateful. When other children might have turned their disappointment into anger, when we might have learned to disrespect the man who couldn't come home, Mommie wouldn't allow that narrative. She held onto hope, and so did we.

Christmas after Christmas, we believed this might be the year. Visit after visit, we treasured the time we had. Promise after promise, we chose to believe rather than doubt.

If we had given up on Daddy, if we'd let disappointment curdle into hatred, we might have grown up with a fundamental disrespect for him—and by extension, a broken understanding of family, love, and the complexity of trying to do right under impossible circumstances. But Mommie's grace prevented that. Her refusal to let us blame him, her own sustained hope even as the marriage gradually dissolved, her insistence that we hold onto love rather than anger—that was its own kind of resistance against Jim Crow's design.

The Jim Crow system didn't just want to separate fathers from families physically. It wanted to destroy the love, to poison the memory, to make children hate their fathers for failing them. That psychological destruction would have been the final victory.

Hope saved us. We denied Jim Crow that victory.

I understand now what I couldn't as a twelve-year-old: Daddy was the supportive family man we remembered, *and* he couldn't overcome the forces arrayed against him. Both things are true. The cognitive dissonance we felt—How could the man who loved us leave and not come back?—wasn't confusion about who he was. That was the collision between his love for us and the systemic impossibility of expressing that love the way he wanted to. He was, indeed, a family man.

He didn't fail us. He was failed by a system designed to ensure that men like him—Black, capable, loving, trying—couldn't win no matter what they chose.

The tragedy wasn't that he didn't love us enough. The tragedy was that Jim Crow made love insufficient to overcome systemic barriers. That a mother's rational calculation about her children's survival had to override a father's desire to reunite his family. That nine children had to grow up with an absent father not because he abandoned them, but because the system made his presence economically impossible.

We held onto hope because Mommie taught us to. We held onto love because she modeled it. We held onto respect for a man who faced impossible choices because she refused to let bitterness take root.

That might be one of the most important things Mommie gave us: not just survival through the ups and downs of the civil rights movement, not just preparation to march and organize and stand up for justice, but the ability to hold complexity, to understand that people we love can be caught in circumstances beyond their control, to refuse the easy narrative of blame when the real culprit is systemic oppression.

Years later, understanding the full picture—the PTSD, the gambling, the economic trap, the impossible distance—I'm grateful we never gave up on our dad. Because the alternative would have meant carrying a different kind of wound into adulthood: the wound of hating someone who deserved our compassion, of blaming someone who was himself a victim, of letting Jim Crow's design complete its psychological destruction of our family.

We didn't allow that to happen. Mommie didn't allow that to happen.

Given hindsight, I now have the clarity to recognize what was simply another way we children—Selma's foot soldiers—were prepared for what would come. We learned early on that love can work alongside disappointment, hope can survive empty promises, and understanding means looking beyond hurt to see larger factors at play.

Those lessons would serve us well when, not many years later, we walked across the Edmund Pettus Bridge on Bloody Sunday.

When word arrived in 1970 that Clarence Sr. had died in Cleveland, his children's grief was mixed with sorrow caused by years of separation and unresolved emotions. Two weeks before his death, he had made a tape-recorded message to his children, which Gwendolyn played for the family when she came home for Christmas. The message was both a gift and a source of additional sadness, revealing that he had still loved them and thought of them constantly but reminding them all of the conversations they'd never be able to have.

"Everyone's going to have to step up now," Carrie told her children the evening after our father left for Cleveland the second time. Ten-year-old Gwendolyn, eight-year-old Carolyn, seven-year-old Yolanda, six-year-old Joan, and four-year-old twins Frederick and I all gathered around the dining table, trying to process what this change would mean for our daily lives.

"That doesn't mean you're not kids anymore," she went on, seeing the concern on their faces. "It means we're going to take better care of each other, and everybody is going to pitch in in the ways that fit what they can do."

The job shift occurred naturally over the following weeks. Gwendolyn, as the oldest, took on increased authority over her younger siblings, helping to organize morning routines of getting up and dressing for school, and in the evenings making sure homework was completed. Carolyn became the primary helper for cooking meals and kitchen cleanup. Yolanda and Joan shared responsibility for keeping the younger children entertained and out of trouble.

But most of all, we developed a deep understanding of how to adjust our schedules and our expectations to fit around our mother's work obligations. We knew that when she went out for a delivery, we had to operate independently until she came back. We learned to support each other through problems that would have once demanded adult intervention.

"When Mommie's not here, Gwen is in charge." That became the household rule number one. "Rule number two: When Gwen's not here, Carolyn is in charge. Everyone takes care of everyone younger than them."

This system worked because the children had been raised from an early age to understand that our family's life was not like other families. We had grown up watching our mother nurse the community, understanding that her work was vital and that their own needs sometimes had to wait for medical emergencies to be resolved.

The house on 1421 Sylvan Street had become much more than a family home. It now stood as proof that strength in the family could withstand adversity and that communities would rally to uphold their most precious members during trying moments. It also proved that children raised with love, responsibility, and high expectations could exceed everyone's assumptions of what they were capable of achieving.

Baby Sherman, arriving in 1958, brought joy and new complications to the smooth working domestic systems on Sylvan Street. A seventh child meant changes in sleeping arrangements, meal planning, and the precise choreography that got everybody prepared for school each day. But it also meant something wonderful for Carrie: a new baby to love and care for, with the family uniting around that responsibility of raising their newest member.

"This baby's going to be all of ours," Carrie told the children as they joined around her to meet their new brother. "Everybody's going to help take care of him, and he's going to grow up knowing that he has six older siblings who love him."

The older children were thrilled to have this responsibility. Gwendolyn, who was eleven at the time, would become Sherman's second mother-in-training, changing his wet diaper and helping him to quit crying. Five-year-old twins Frederick and I appointed ourselves his entertainment committee; we knew just how to make him laugh with a few faces or silly noises that always made babies smile.

But Sherman's arrival also exposed the financial burden that single parenthood had placed on the household. Seven children needed more of everything—food, clothes, medical attention, school supplies. Carrie's clinic pay, which had been steady over the years, suddenly had to stretch further than ever before.

This was when the community safety net stepped up in full force. Neighbors who, for years, had been recipients of Carrie's medical care began finding ways to help in return. Mrs. Sallie would often appear on Fridays with extra food from the cafeteria. The barber would cut the boys' hair, and his wife, a beautician, would cut and style the girls' hair, all free of charge. Mr. Charlie White from three doors down would offer to do household repairs without her asking him to, knowing that Carrie's budget couldn't accommodate both professional services and the basic needs of a family. Whenever they needed plumbing repairs, Mr. Ernest Parnell, the neighbor who had a plumbing business and lived directly across from them, stopped in to offer his services. "Neighbors help neighbors," he said. "You fix people when they're sick, I fix pipes when they act up."

"We look out for each other around here," Mrs. Coleman told a newcomer in the neighborhood who questioned why everyone was so ready to help the Jones family. "Mrs. Carrie's helped take care of us all these years. Now it's our turn to make sure she and those kids have what they need." This social care ran throughout all aspects of life, even how the children spent their after-school and weekend hours.

When systemic injustices pushed our father out of our home, our resilient community stepped up to fill the void. As the families in our neighborhood always did, we supported each other through the toughest times. This system of mutual support made Carrie's medical work possible, and it would become the backbone of our involvement in the civil rights movement.

CHAPTER FIVE

Bringing Life

I love making people happy—my mother loved making people happy also. Thank you, God, again, for this day.

—Carrie Louise, Dec. 13, 1998

The call came at 2:30 in the morning in February 1954. It was a cold winter night with stars that seemed only inches away. Carrie sat up, suddenly awoken when pebbles clacked against her window from the alley below. This was the signal that someone urgently required her services.

"Mrs. Carrie! Mrs. Carrie!" a whispered voice called from the yard beneath. "It's Mrs. Johnson's time, and she's calling for you!"

Within minutes, Carrie was dressing and picking up the leather medical bag that she now never left behind: clean linens, towels, and the portable equipment that allowed her to turn any bedroom into a safe delivery room. She had slipped silently through the house, checking on her sleeping children and leaving a note for Clarence on where she'd gone and when he could expect to see her again.

The path this early morning was by now a familiar one, a route she had taken hundreds of times in the last decade through Selma's predawn streets. Her feet learned every bend in the sidewalk, every loose board on all of those porches, every shortcut that could save precious minutes when time was a matter of life and death. The bag with her equipment gently swung at her side, holding instruments and medication, while her head carried the collected wisdom of safely bringing new life into the world.

Mrs. Johnson lived six blocks away in a small house Carrie had frequented for prenatal checkups during the pregnancy. It would be Mrs. Johnson's fourth child, and that meant the labor was going to proceed rapidly once it got going in earnest. But fourth babies could also be ornery, and Carrie had been taught never to take any childbirth for granted.

Unsurprisingly, Mrs. Johnson was walking around the tiny living room, one hand pressed against her lower back and the other encircling her husband's arm as another contraction ramped up to its peak. Mrs. Johnson's mother and sister were there; so was Mrs. Coleman from next door. This web of women knew that life was intensely personal and innately communal too.

"Feelin' them contractions for how long now?" asked Carrie, setting her bag on the floor and washing her hands in one of the basins that had been provided alongside some toiletries.

"Once every five minutes for the past hour," said Mrs. Johnson's mother. "Getting stronger each time."

"And the water?"

"Broke about twenty minutes ago. That's when we sent for you."

Carrie nodded, already moving into the gathering, exuding the competent presence that women in labor needed to see. She examined her patient carefully, determined the baby's position, monitored the progression of labor, and assessed whether this delivery would proceed normally or need intervention.

"So far, everything looks good," she declared. "Baby's head down, and you're what we call favorable. This little fella is ready to meet you tonight."

For the next four hours, Carrie coached Mrs. Johnson through the labor stages she knew as well as her own pulse. She watched over both mother and baby, offered reassurance and encouragement, and kept track of the myriad details that determined whether a delivery was safe or perilous.

"I can't do this anymore," Mrs. Johnson cried during one acutely painful contraction. "It hurts too much."

"You can, yes you can," Carrie said, holding Mrs. Johnson's hands and staring her in the eyes. "Your body prepares the way for you, and you are stronger than you believe yourself to be. And this baby is going to be right here, and then you're not even gonna remember this pain."

This was the point when average midwives were separated from good ones because they offered not just expertise in medical supervision and processes, but the kind of spiritual support that could help women find courage at a time when courage seemed absent altogether. Carrie came to understand that delivering a baby was not only a matter of medical science, but the faith she offered to each family, and she knew that sometimes more than anything else, what made the difference in a delivery was her certainty that mother and child would emerge intact.

When the baby had at last come—a bouncing, healthy boy who let the room know of his arrival with bold cries of indignation—the small bedroom was brimming with the sort of joy that made everyone there remember why this work was sacred. Carrie wiped down the sweet little naked newborn, checking him all over before she wrapped him up in soft blankets and put him into his mother's arms.

"He's perfect," Mrs. Johnson whispered, touching her son's small fingers and basking in the end of the nine-month journey.

"He sure is," Carrie said, already tidying up and readying herself for a few hours of cautious observation. The delivery was over, but her treatment wasn't through until she knew the mother and her baby were stable and that any complications had been identified and resolved.

That is how Carrie's nights went in the 1950s, over and over again: a knock at her door, then urgent calls to make quick preparations, to attend one of life's most elemental events—with that deep satisfaction professionals feel when they help families through a safe transition from pregnancy to parenthood. Each birth was different; each woman carried her own fears and power into the experience, but the basic aspects of it were constant: preparedness, skill, presence, and faith.

It was dawn when the Selma girl finally walked home through the sleepy streets of the awakening town, and with her more than just tiredness from hours of strained concentration—she carried a deep sense of fulfillment. Another family was whole, another baby had been born fit and strong, and another woman had found strength she never knew existed.

At 1421 Sylvan Street, the family was awakening as Carrie walked up. The older children would be getting ready for school, baby Sherman waking up hungry, and the routine of family life going on as usual. But for a little bit there, standing in her front yard and watching smoke billow out from chimneys all up and down the block, Carrie claimed that moment of quiet satisfaction from a job well done.

This work is what she had been summoned to do; to not just practice medicine but to be a part of the miracle of new life. Not only to contribute to the community, but also to help make certain that its future arrives safe and equipped with the best start in life.

The trust Carrie built from hundreds of successful deliveries was not only due to medical care but was also based on the network she traveled through. Those who had shared in her wise and loving presence at the birth of their own children now spread the word among friends, relatives, and acquaintances struggling with pregnancies of their own.

"You have to get Mrs. Carrie to deliver that baby," was a common piece of advice women shared with expectant mothers throughout Selma's colored community. "She's competent and she'll take care of you when your time comes."

This trust was not only grounded in technical expertise, though Carrie was a talented nurse. It was founded on her belief that birth was more than delivering safe and healthy babies—it was about being with women as they birthed, in what could be one of life's most profound experiences, asking women to honor this sacred rite, and making sure families felt supported during their most vulnerable time.

Mrs. Williams learned this lesson in trying circumstances during one spring day in 1955, amid a difficult delivery. Her baby was the wrong way 'round, a problem that would take all of Carrie's expertise to rectify without it being dangerous for the mother. For six hours, Carrie slowly massaged and manipulated the slippery flesh to turn the baby and help Mrs. Williams with a labor that called on both women's endurance and faith.

"I can't do this," said Mrs. Williams in a whisper during one especially tough period. "We might need to get Dr. Dumont."

"We will if we have to," Carrie responded evenly, "but your baby is good right now and everything in your body is functioning just as it should. Trust yourself, trust the birthing process, and then just trust me to stay right here with you until that little one comes out safely."

The baby who arrived at last was a strong, healthy girl who would eventually become one of the first colored nurses to receive training in a Northern hospital. "You not only caught my baby," she would tell Carrie weeks later. "You taught me what I was capable of. I'll never forget that."

These bonds of shared intensity in labor and delivery were enduring. Women whom Carrie had supported during childbirth formed part of an informal reciprocal assistance network that in turn bolstered the entire community. They pooled resources when times were tough, took care of each other's kids in emergencies, and offered the kind of emotional comfort that helped families scrape by even under difficult conditions. This mutual aid was vital in a community where Jim Crow segregation barred Black women from the mainstream medical care and social support systems built for white mothers.

The realism of midwifery also meant that Carrie, like her mother Hettie, learned to be a masterful organizer and scheduler in order to serve a community that lacked resources like reliable transportation. She learned to pack enough stuff for whatever situation she found herself in, to efficiently work in homes that didn't have electricity or running water, and to make life-or-death decisions based on how she intuited the unique needs of each situation.

Some nights, though, she would be called to homes where the right preparations had been made—clean sheets, hot water, a proper lighting source, and family who knew how to help during delivery. Other nights she would walk in and see cups of coffee left cold, and a mounting panic from five or more women there to support the birthing mother, all of whom felt unprepared.

"Don't worry about what you don't have," she would tell families who appeared embarrassed by their lot. "I have what I need, and babies have been born safely in much worse circumstances than this. We can concentrate on the important things, like bringing your little one out safely."

This no-nonsense outlook applied to her pain management and treatment as well. In the days before epidurals and sophisticated pain relievers, the episodes she guided through those rooms often demanded coping mechanisms such as positioning and breathing patterns, not to mention a kind of emotional encouragement that allowed women to work with their bodies rather than against them. Carrie knew when to rush for help and when patience and encouragement were the best medicine.

But most of all, she knew that midwifery was as much about caring for families as it was about catching babies. After the birth, she would remain with new mothers for hours, overseeing their recovery, helping them initiate breastfeeding, and teaching and reassuring new parents about what to expect as they cared for newborns.

At 1421 Sylvan Street, midwifery gave the day its rhythm just as much as any other factor. The challenges of building such a huge midwifery business while at the same time rearing nine children necessitated constant change and innovation. Carrie created systems of time, materials, and energy management that helped her meet the needs of the community while also meeting her family's needs.

The children adapted to sleeping through late-night departures and early-morning returns. They knew that dinnertime, homework time, and times for all the little things a family at least intends to do together could be called aside when Mommie was summoned.

"Where's Mommie?" was now a standard question among Carrie's children, a question normally answered by whoever the older child in charge that day happened to be.

"Mrs. Rawls is having a baby. Mommie will be back when baby comes."

The older children learned to run the household while she was gone, handling their chores efficiently. They could cook meals and help younger kids with homework; they could deal with small crises, enforce discipline, and keep the family running like a machine. This was not just practical necessity—it was practice for their active roles during the civil rights movement.

"We're not just learning how to take care of ourselves," Gwendolyn said one evening as she helped her younger siblings with homework while Carrie delivered twins across town. "We're learning how to take care of our community."

The dynamic was challenging at times, but the children were proud of their mother's work and that they could help support it. They grew more self-reliant than their peers, more likely to help one another with problems instead of farming issues out for parental intervention, and they came to see that the life of their family revolved around service to others. This consciousness—of no distinction between personal responsibility and community service—would become the stable base for everything that they would build on in their lives.

When baby Sherman turned out to be a particularly fussy eater who would not abide eating the grits that had sustained all his older brothers and sisters, Carrie found ways to try and accommodate him without making special allowances that would disrupt family routines. Breakfast cereal was slightly more expensive than grits, but she found a way to make it fit into the budget, partly because ensuring that each child had enough to eat was part of her work as both a mother and trained medical professional.

"Every child is different," she told the older children, who wanted to know why Sherman got cereal when they had always eaten grits. "Part of taking care of people is paying attention to what each individual needs, not treating everybody exactly the same."

This lesson in individualized care was one that the children would carry with them throughout their lives. Carrie's example taught them that what is really fair has to do with doing for people based on their needs, rather than trying to apply a one-size-fits-all response.

Into the 1950s, Carrie's midwifery practice broadened from central Selma to encompass families in outlying rural areas near the city. These calls usually involved longer walks or rides in whatever mode of transportation could be secured, taking her into areas where poverty was still more desperate and medical resources even scarcer.

One winter night in 1956, she was summoned to deliver a baby for a family that lived in a sharecropper's cabin fifteen miles outside Selma. The old truck of Mr. Charlie White was the only conveyance to be had, and it jolted noisily over rain-muddied trails as old creaky barns swayed in the wind, jeering at the truck's progress.

"Are you sure you want to go out in this weather?" Mr. Charlie asked, chugging through another muddy rut. "Roads like this, we might not get back before morning."

"Baby won't wait for clearer skies," Carrie responded, reviewing her gear bag to ensure its contents had been secured against the truck's jolting. "And this woman's already had three miscarriages. She needs somebody who knows what they're doing."

After receiving directions from a passing drifter, they finally arrived at the cabin, which was a one-room building with enough space between the wallboards to see daylight. The pregnant, not-yet-nineteen-year-old mother-to-be worked her labor over a mattress on wooden slats. Her husband and mother-in-law stood nearby, plainly scared by their responsibility to usher a new life in such dire circumstances.

"Everything's going to be fine," Carrie proclaimed as she opened her supplies by the glow of two kerosene lamps. "This isn't the worst situation I've delivered a baby in. Let's listen to what your body is telling us and get this little one here safely."

The delivery went well, but in the aftermath, it became evident just how much help the family needed. The cabin had no running water, virtually no food supplies, and totally inadequate heating for an Alabama winter. The new mother was weak from malnutrition in pregnancy, and the baby, while healthy, wasn't as big as he should've been.

"Mrs. Carrie," the young father said as she got ready to leave, "I can't pay you very much money. Misery is easy enough for most people in this part of the state right now; cotton didn't bring what we hoped, and times have been bad."

"You give what you can, when you can," Carrie answered. "Right now, you concentrate on your wife and that beautiful baby."

But Carrie also mentally listed follow-up care that would be needed: postnatal visits to check on mother and baby, a referral to the pediatric service at Dr. Dumont's clinic, and community resources that might address other family needs.

These rural calls taught Carrie that midwifery was not just about a safe delivery; it was about babies going into families that were going to be able to nurture and support them. Sometimes that meant delivering medical care, sometimes it meant connecting families with resources, and often it just meant giving hope and encouragement to people who faced impossible odds in a segregated world.

Back in Selma, the difference between families was just as stark. Some births took place in well-furnished homes where meticulous preparations had been made and resources were plentiful. Others occurred within crowded homes where several families lived, making privacy scarce.

But no matter what, Carrie treated every single delivery with the highest level of professional skill and personal care. She believed the moment of birth was a sanctum, regardless of whether it was happening in comfort or poverty. Every child had a right to enter life caught by loving, capable hands.

There was a heavy emotional price to be paid for this work, but the cost was bearable because of the fulfillment that came with it. Each successful birth was a win, not just for the individual family, but for the greater community. Every healthy baby was hope for the future, evidence that even in an atmosphere of segregation, even in the teeth of economic deprivation, life went on and families grew.

"You know the best thing for me in this job?" said Carrie one day when she was chewing over the week's deliveries with Dr. Dumont. "It's about beginnings. Each baby is hope, potentiality. In a world that's constantly telling our children they are constrained, each birth tells us that the future is still unwritten."

This philosophy also applied to how she spoke with expectant parents about their dreams and hopes for their children. She wanted them to dream beyond the limitations that segregation tried to define, to believe their children could accomplish things that may have seemed impossible under their dire conditions.

"This baby could be a doctor someday," she'd tell parents as she lay newborns in their arms. "Or a teacher, or a lawyer, or anything else they dare to dream up. The world is moving, and your child is going to be a part of that movement."

It was as if those words were more than comfort, full of prophecy. In fact, many of the babies born to Carrie in the 1950s would go on to do amazing things as professionals: Several would complete college studies and become community leaders and advocates for change. Carrie believed that every child had a boundless capacity no society could predict or order. This conviction fostered a generation unwilling to accept the limits their society tried to put on them because of their skin color, social station, or any other identifying factor.

Many of the most difficult calls came in Selma's sweltering summers, when heat made labor more difficult and raised women's risk of complications. In July 1958, one woman's pregnancy showed how dangerous these high-heat labors could be. Mrs. Sarah Davis, aged thirty-seven or thirty-eight years, was the mother of five children whose most recent pregnancy had occurred several years earlier.

The little house was oppressively hot, even in the middle of the night when Carrie was called in, though every window and door stood open for whatever breeze might blow. Mrs. Davis was spent before labor had truly begun, fatigued by the heat and the exertion of caring for five other children while working to help support her family.

"I am too old for this," she gasped between contractions. "My body isn't responding to this the way I expect."

"Your body remembers what to do," Carrie coached her, applying cool, damp cloths to help cope with the heat and track the baby's progress. "With age comes knowledge, and knowledge can make you stronger, not weaker."

But privately, Carrie was concerned. The labor was sluggish, Mrs. Davis was growing weaker and the heat rendered everything harder to bear. This was precisely the type of situation in which her relationship with Dr. Dumont had been invaluable, having medical support on hand if something went wrong and escalated beyond what Carrie had been trained to handle.

"Mrs. Davis, I want Dr. Dumont to come take a look," she said after several hours of little progress. "Not because anything's wrong, but because I want to make sure we have all our options available."

Receiving medical consultation was never an easy call to make. It was to concede that a situation was beyond the range of midwifery care. Yet it also represented the professional judgment that protected mothers and babies. Within an hour, Dr. Dumont arrived, examined the patient, and decided there must be a medical case.

"We have to take her to the hospital," whispered Dr. Dumont. "The baby is distressed, and the mother is too tired to keep laboring safely at home."

Carrie and Dr. Dumont performed the transfer to Good Samaritan Hospital expediently, and mother and baby both recovered from what could have been a tragic moment. But the experience also solidified in Carrie how important it was to know not only how to support normal births, but when circumstances demanded more resources than home birth could offer.

"You got it just right," Dr. Dumont would tell her later. "Learning when to ask for help is as important as knowing how to handle things on your own. That's what saved Mrs. Davis and her baby."

Those experiences handling difficult medical situations while being the trusted ally of concerned families only enhanced Carrie's burgeoning reputation as a woman who could be counted on in any situation. Word got out that not only could she safely deliver babies, but that she had the judgment to know when to ask for help and the professional connections to secure it.

The effect of Carrie's midwifery practice on her own family was profound. The fees she earned for deliveries, while small, brought in vital extra money to put food on the table for nine children on a single mother's income. But even more than the money was a trade and barter system that emerged around her services.

Carrie learned from watching Dr. Dumont accept nonmonetary payment from patients at her clinic, and from her mother Hettie's give- and-take with goods and services among neighbors on and around Saint Ann Street. Those families who couldn't come up with cash for Carrie's in-home midwifery and other medical services would instead contribute produce from their gardens, labor on household repairs, babysitting services, or other forms of support that minimized the Jones family's costs. Mr. Lump, who lived across the street, regularly shared fish from his fishing trips—Carrie had delivered two of his grandchildren. The school cafeteria manager and her daughter made it a habit to save any leftover food on Fridays instead of throwing it out, knowing nine children would be waiting on Sylvan Street.

"We got each other's back," grew to become the unofficial motto of the network of families that connected through Carrie's work in the community. Like the web of mothers whom Carrie had served as midwife, this broader collective support network became a kind of safety net that helped everyone get through the economic turmoil of segregation-era Alabama.

By 1959, when Carrie gave birth to her second set of twins Christopher and Anthony, she had delivered over two hundred babies without losing a mother or child. This remarkable track record owed much not only to her medical talents, but to a recognition that successful midwifery also meant caring about every aspect of another woman's health and life.

As the 1950s drew to a close and the civil rights movement began to heat up across the South, the network that Carrie built through her work as a midwife was about to be uniquely vital in ways no one could have foreseen. The trust she built, the relationships she developed, and her reputation would be assets when her young children got involved in activities aimed at breaking down a segregated status quo.

The children who lived at 1421 Sylvan Street had long known that their mother's job was about more than making money; it was about serving their community in its darkest moments. They had grown to accept that they would have to modify their schedules and expectations around emergency calls, be proud of their mother for her reputation, and see themselves as part of a greater mission related to service and care.

"Mommie helps deliver babies," was how they told friends about their family's unique situation. These were simple words that said something profound. Carrie's children were part of something bigger than just their family, and that purpose extended to the other families throughout their community and beyond.

The house at 1421 Sylvan Street had evolved into a classroom and incubator for a practice of giving that would touch hundreds of lives, build networks of mutual support that provided strength to the whole community, and prove daily that service to others could be both profession and calling.

CHAPTER SIX

The Days of Pea Shelling Parties

The end of summer always made its appearance the same way in Selma—by the rumble down Sylvan Street, loaded high with bushels of purple hull peas, crowder peas, and whatever else had been harvested that year from the sharecropper's land across the river in Brantley. The sight of that truck meant just one thing to the kids at 1421 Sylvan Street: Pea shelling party time had arrived.

"Y'all come help me pile these bushels out back," Carrie would call, emerging from the house with an energy level and organizational ability that turned what could have been a lot of very overwhelming work for just one or two people into more like a community party. "And somebody run tell Ms. Emma and Mrs. Coleman we're having a party today."

The backyard at 1421 Sylvan Street was about to change, as if by magic. Uncle John's elaborate barbecue pit would be started up, not for cooking just yet, but because smoke was known to scare off mosquitoes for the long afternoon of work that lay ahead. Folding chairs and kitchen chairs would come from houses next door and across the street, all set up in a rough circle beneath the shade of the pecan tree. Giant basins and bowls would be handed out for the towering mounds of shells that would pile up while everyone took part in what was a work session, social gathering, and a community bonding rite all rolled into one.

"Now keep in mind," Carrie would say to the assembled crowd of relatives and neighbors, "we're all working together here. Everyone keeps working until everyone's bushel is completed. That's how we ensure that everybody can go home with enough to make it till spring."

The cast of characters changed from year to year, but the inner circle never did. Both Ms. Emma and Mrs. Coleman came over from next door, knowing full well that helping to shell the peas earned them a stake in the finished product. Aunt Marzetta would be there, along with Aunt Lizzie if she wasn't working at the hospital, and whatever cousins had come in from out of town at the moment. But always there in the middle of it all was Hettie, the grand matriarch whose presence raised any gathering above plain old work to a family tradition.

"Hand me that bushel of butter beans," Hettie might instruct, leaning back in her chair with the assurance of someone who had been orchestrating those meets for years. "These young folks don't even know how to shell beans right, half 'a the good on the outside of their pods."

The rhythm of the work induced something like a trance—hands flew open and shut, splitting the feathery pods by instinct and then emptying them into bowls, while conversations circled back to where they had begun, or leapt from subject to subject like water left on its own to find a passage. Neighborhood news, church gossip, worries about children, progress reports on family members who had moved to the North—it all revolved around the practical business of taking care of one another.

"Mrs. Johnson's baby is finally sleeping through the night," they'd report.

"Mr. Charlie's mother is sick again. Someone should check on her."

"The Patterson boy landed that job at the brickyard. His mama's so proud."

These were the conversations by which information moved around the community, problems identified before they became crises and solutions developed collaboratively rather than in isolation. These pea shelling parties were really not parties at all but meetings of neighbors who congregated to support one another.

We drifted in and out of the circle, sometimes pulling up a chair to help with shelling if only briefly each day, sometimes playing around the yard, but always soaking up the lessons about cooperation and generosity and honoring connections within a community. We were taught that work could be social, that helping others was just what you did, and that when things were abundant, you didn't hoard them, but shared instead.

"Y'all are learning something important today," Mrs. Coleman said to ten-year-old Gwendolyn, who sat with great concentration, shelling peas around the adults. "You're learning that we look out for each other around here. That's what families do, and that's what neighbors do."

The pile of shelled peas would grow and the pile of empty bushel baskets would dwindle as the afternoon dragged on. Stories were shared, guidance given, plans created, and the strong ties that bound us as a community only grew stronger simply by working alongside each other towards one common goal.

Once the final pod had been shelled and the peas portioned, it was time to clean up, another communal task that reflected the same ethos of joint responsibility. Chairs would be hauled back to their proper places, washbasins washed and carried out, and everyone would head home with sacks full of peas that were not just food for the winter but a symbol of community solidarity.

But the pea shelling parties were only one of those instances in which seasonal rhythms organized community life around mutual assistance and shared plenty. When peaches, apricots, and berries were brought to the city from relatives in the country by Uncle William's truck, Carrie would put on "jamming parties" which carried out the same principle: Work all together and then share in the results.

The jamming parties used a different skill set and different tools than pea shelling, but the social dynamics remained consistent. Women would converge on Carrie's kitchen, taking turns at the stove stirring large pots of fruit and sugar while others sterilized and readied Mason jars and lids for canning. The whole house would be filled with the sweet scent of boiling fruit and steam rising from many pots on the go at once.

"The whole secret of proper preserves," Hettie would declare, "is just knowing when your fruit is ready to set up proper. Too little and it's runny, too much and it becomes tough. You have to watch it real close and trust your eye."

Those lessons in food preservation were also lessons in planning, on turning temporary abundance into the assurance of year-round bounty. The rows of mason jars of fig preserves, peach jam, and berry jelly her mother had lined up along the shelves in Carrie's pantry were no more an act of vanity than they were folly; rather, they secured insurance against the lean months when fresh fruit was dear or unavailable.

But as with the pea shelling, the jamming parties made more than just preserved food. They were opportunities for women to pass on knowledge, provide support, and build relationships that would be vital in the hard times that often characterized the segregated American South. Young girls learned household tasks, mothers were relieved of child-rearing chores, and all derived a sense of accomplishment from productive communal labor. Carrie instructed her daughters in the art and science of jelly, jam, and preserve-making—Hettie's instruction trickling down another generation. The children learned what fruits they could combine, how much sugar and pectin various fruits need, how to determine when preserves have cooked long enough to set up properly, and how to size jars for safe storage.

And wasn't the fig tree in the backyard of 1421 Sylvan Street a seasonal source of preservation and sharing? At fig-ripening time each summer, generally just prior to the pea shelling parties, Carrie would put on mini-parties to turn that fruit into preserves which graced breakfast tables until well through wintertime.

In Carrie's house, "Nothing beats fig preserves and Mommie's biscuits" became a family saying that expressed not only appreciation for good food but an awareness of the care and planning that made such bounty possible, even on a tight budget.

This meant there was never just plain toast at 1421 Sylvan Street. Even the most ordinary of breakfasts were a celebration on those days when we had homemade jam on the table, and just as satisfying to the girls was the pride they felt that they were providing something for our grandparents' table. During her most resource-strapped moments, Carrie would spread butter on bread and then sprinkle it with brown sugar and cinnamon before toasting; the small extravagance cost next to nothing yet made children feel pampered instead of deprived.

The process of meat preservation was different but followed the same communal spirit. From the east side of the Alabama River, seasonal gifts would come from Sugar Boy, one of Carrie's country cousins. He'd show up each autumn with a nice portion of a butchered hog already conveniently cut into storage size and wrapped in white waxed freezer paper. Chops, hams, and bacon stowed ready for the winter, another example of how family networks made sure everyone got their share of protein, even if personal budgets couldn't stretch to include such luxuries.

These seasonal kitchen rituals were teaching us children fundamentals that went well beyond the mechanics of preserving food. We learned that abundance was only for a while, and, if properly managed, can provide security when times were lean. Personal success, we discovered, is less valuable than community health, and work can be joyful if done in the company of people you loved.

Most importantly, we discovered that survival isn't antithetical to celebration; the utilitarian task of making sure everyone had enough to eat could also be generative of its own kind of story, relationships, and community. The pea shelling parties and jamming sessions were, all at the same time, economic necessity and social celebration, practical work and cultural preservation.

"This is how we've done it for years," Hettie would tell us as they watched the adults work together in casual, easy harmony. "People had to find ways of preserving food and sharing with neighbors long before there were stores where you could buy everything you needed. I grew up in those times and with these skills. These skills kept our families alive, and they'll keep you alive too if you pay attention and learn."

These family events also exposed us to friendships between adults as well as how communities worked. We noticed how disagreements were addressed diplomatically, how resources were shared fairly, and how work was distributed as people's abilities or availability dictated. We discovered that leadership was about taking responsibility for organizing and coordinating but not simply issuing orders.

As us children got older, we started to chip in with the work of these seasonal meet-ups. The older girls were taught how to time canning precisely, and us boys learned how to transport heavy bushels and keep tools in working order for large-scale food preservation.

Much like preserving food, music also taught us important truths about community and ingenuity. The summer when Carrie's first set of twins, Frederick and I, were around eight, she made a decision that illustrated her dedication to doing right by her children. She sent Yolanda, Frederick, and me for the summer to live with her Aunt Bessie in Birmingham, whose daughter CB was a piano teacher.

"I want to have you three learn to play piano," she declared, even though there was no money in the household budget for music lessons in Selma. "Cousin CB has agreed to teach you, and you'll board with her over the summer."

The summer in Birmingham had its own difficulties. Cousin CB was a strict teacher and difficult to live with. She punished Frederick and me for a forgotten incident by having us sit on the front porch the whole day, wearing girls' clothes, something neither of us would ever forget.

Uncle Larry gave Frederick and me a different kind of introduction to the power of music. Good-ole Uncle Larry was Carrie's youngest brother, not much older than her.oldest daughters. He was a drummer, rocked the high school marching band, and played with a local group of musicians called the Micronites. He always called us "Carrie's children," and he knew that opportunities had to be created, not waited for.

One summer day, he stopped over at 1421 Sylvan Street with two instruments in a case: a drum and sticks for Frederick and a bass horn for me. He also had already talked to the high school band director about incorporating us into the marching band even though we were still in grade school.

"You boys are going to learn to play," he declared, with that certainty adults have of practical matters having been solved. "Did I tell you that as the lead drummer, I have some clout with the band teacher?"

This act of kindness redeemed the sour summer piano excursion in Birmingham, and it would have implications far beyond Selma. When our family eventually relocated to Georgia, Frederick and I would be ready to walk right into the school's marching band, having learned not just musical skills but also the rigorous discipline of a marching performance.

The bass horn was pretty heavy for a twelve-year-old, and making clear notes required the control of my breath and the mouthpiece to a degree that pushed my physical abilities. But Uncle Larry's confidence in his nephews' potential made the work feel worthwhile, and the chance to collaborate with high school students helped broaden both of our horizons to a world of opportunity just beyond our grasp.

"Music teaches you things that you can't learn any other way," Uncle Larry assured them as they labored over their first lessons. "It forces you to learn discipline, timing and coordination with a group, and how to be something larger than yourself. Those teachings will be invaluable to you no matter what you wind up doing."

In the late 1950s, by which time the civil rights movement was ramping up throughout the South, the sort of network of mutual aid and community cooperation worked out through years of pea shelling parties and jam sessions would become more important than anyone could have predicted. People who worked for civil rights flowed together with mutual support and encouragement, like the members of a marching band moving in lock step and complementing each other's notes and rhythms. Those same webs of trust and reciprocity that ensured everyone had more than enough preserved food to tide them over winter would also provide the infrastructure for families whose breadwinners would be targeted with economic reprisals in response to any civil rights activism.

The same ethic of shared-sacrifice-and-mutual-gain that had

determined the allocation of shelled peas would determine who, in each domestic sphere, could bear to take a chance boycotting or marching, and whose soldiering families needed "fortification" to avoid economic reprisals for their refusal to accept segregation.

This communal protection and solidarity became even more vital when white supremacist terrorism occurred in retaliation for civil rights advances. When I was ten years old, Yolanda, Joan, Frederick, and I were across the street from home at the Parnell's house, where we had come to watch the Cassius Clay boxing match with Sonny Liston on the family's makeshift color television—the kind with colored film paper placed over the screen to simulate color broadcasting. We had been there only a short while when the noise of a loudspeaker and bullhorn drew us to the front porch.

Five or six men wearing white hooded masks over their heads were standing in the back of what looked like a funeral hearse with the back end cut off and opened. There was loud, ugly shouting, and a burning cross standing upright in the middle of the vehicle as it moved slowly down Sylvan Street.

The Ku Klux Klan had brought their message of intimidation and hate directly to the neighborhood where civil rights families lived, a deliberate act of terrorism designed to frighten anyone who might be considering participation in movement activities.

For the children watching from the Parnell's porch, this was our first encounter with the kind of organized hatred that fueled opposition to the civil rights movement. The burning cross, the masked figures, the deliberate choice to parade right through their neighborhood—all of it was meant to create fear and discourage the kind of community organizing that was gaining momentum throughout Selma.

But for now, in the rhythm of spontaneous sufficiency and preservation, the work lay at hand: getting everybody fed, ensuring that knowledge was passed down from one generation to the next, keeping the community support strong enough to ride out whatever came, and continuing to play the song of freedom.

The days of the pea shelling party were about more than just food preservation; they reflected a lifestyle that prioritized cooperation over competition, community over individualism, and shared abundance over private accumulation. And these values would be crucial when the children of 1421 Sylvan Street set out to build American society anew.

Young Nurse Carrie Outside Good Samaritan Hospital.

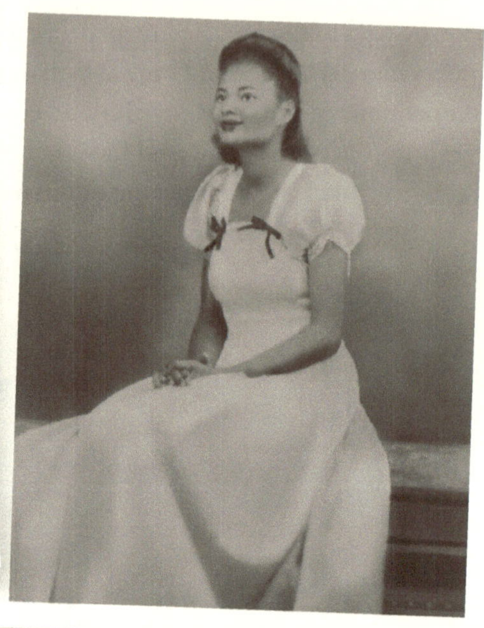

18-year-old Carrie in Prom dress.

1410 Saint Ann Street, Selma, AL, home of Hettie Lundy.

Clarence Sr. in full military dress uniform.

Clarence Sr. in front of WW II ammunitions truck.

Clarence Sr., on far right, with military friends in Europe.

Clarence Sr. on motorcycle alongside ammunitions truck.

Young Uncle Larry in Army dress uniform.

Young Uncle John in Army dress uniform.

Brother Anthony, front row far left, with military paratrooper platoon.

Young Clarence Sr.

Young Clarence Sr.

Young Gwendolyn (r), Carolyn (l), and Yolanda (c), in front of 1421 Sylvan Street.

Young Gwendolyn (b), Carolyn (r), and Joan (l).

Young Carrie with baby Carolyn and little Gwen. Large pecan in background.

Two-year-old twins Clarence (l) and Frederick (r), in Carrie's tailored suits.

Three-year-old twins Clarence (l) and Frederick (r), in Carrie's tailored suits.

Clarence Jr., three-year-old School Day Picture at Hudson High.

Clarence Jr., St. Elizabeth School Picture 2nd Grade.

Carolyn, age 8, School Day Pictures at Saint Elizabeth.

Yolanda, age 7, School Day Pictures at Saint Elizabeth.

Joan, age 4, in Carrie's tailored dress.

Joan, age 6, School Day Pictures at Saint Elizabeth.

Yolanda, age 6, School Day Pictures at Saint Elizabeth.

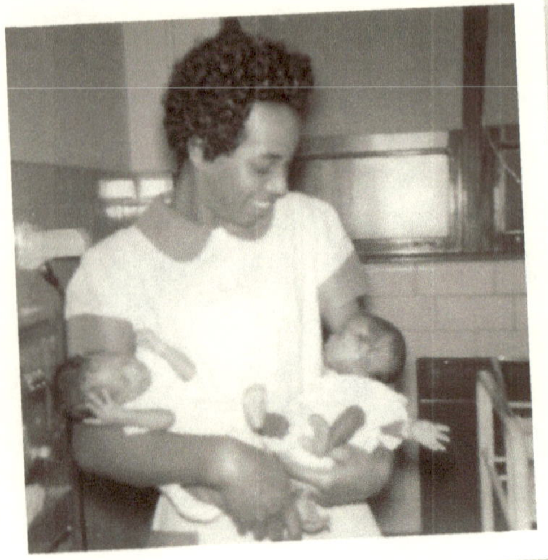

Aunt Lizzie, with in Good Samaritan Premi-Ward with twins Christopher and Anthony.

Young twins Anthony (l) and Christopher (r) in Carrie's home sewn suits.

Young twins Anthony (l) and Christopher (r) in living room of 1421 Sylvan Street.

Young Christopher (l) and Anthony (r) with young adult Carolyn in Atlanta's Grove Park.

Carrie's children's First Holy Communion with Sister Marie Helen and Father Ouelette.

Young Jones siblings in Moss's swimming pool at annual picnic.

Carrie and children at 1421 Sylvan Street Mother's Day celebration.

Carrie and children at Mother's Day celebration. Clarence Jr., Carrie, Yolanda, Nell, Carolyn, Frederick, Gwendolyn, Edrena Parnell, and Joan.

Carrie celebrates Sherman's birthday with cousins and friends.

Carolyn in Fifth Grade group photo outside St. Elizabeth Catholic School.

Young Clarence Jr., in Easter Boycott outfit-overalls and white shirt.

Cousin James Harold in background after 12-ft goal raising. Clarence Jr., and Frederick in foreground right, neighbor left, and young Sherman and Christopher in second row.

Cousin James Harold takes shot after 12-ft goal raising. Clarence Jr., and Frederick in foreground; young twin Christopher and neighbor in background.

Eighth Grade Twins Clarence Jr., and Frederick in Hudson H.S. band uniforms.

Clarence Sr., on night out with oldest daughter, College Freshman Gwendolyn.

Gwendolyn Jones, Senior Year at Holy Rosary Institute.

Clarence Sr., on night out with oldest daughter, College Freshman Gwendolyn.

Gwendolyn, age 19, College Freshman at Cleveland State University.

Young big sister Rubie, receiving outstanding service award at Good Samaritan.

Big sister Rubie, day off from work in first.

Young Adult Carolyn Jones.

Clarence Jr., far right, R.B. Hudson High Junior Varsity winning Basketball Team.

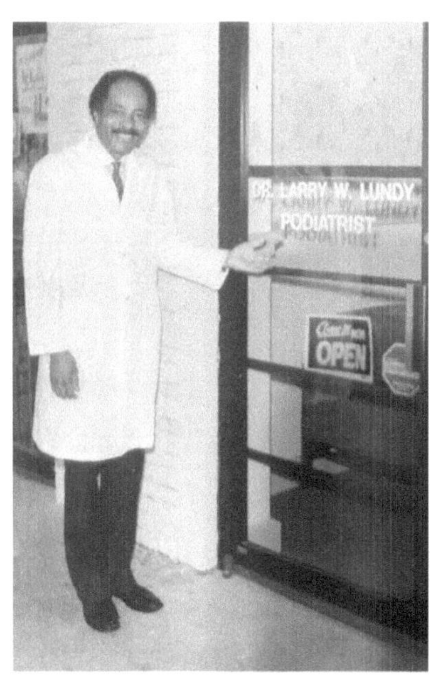

Carrie's oldest brother, Uncle Willie, opening his Podiatry Clinic.

Two-year old Shelia and Jeffrey in Christmas cars.

Carrie's youngest sibling Larry, with local Micronites band.

Hettie Lundy with oldest son Dr. Willie Lundy.

Young Judge Gwendolyn Jones Thomas.

Carrie with her five adult daughters – Gwendolyn, Carolyn, Shelia, Yolanda, and Joan.

Carrie's ten adult children.

Pops, Shelia, and Carrie at Shelia Marie's Graduation.

Shelia Marie Graduation. Shelia, Horace Hunter (Pops), Carrie (second from right).

Apricots and Rhubarb, preserves by Yolanda.

Gumbo soup by Carolyn.

Pizza special, by Yolanda.

Green Street Baptist Church, Selma.

Brown Chapel AME Church, Selma.

Tabernacle Baptist, Selma.

CHAPTER SEVEN

There Goes Carrie's Kids

God said we must love each other, as we love ourselves, meaning love one another as He has loved us.

—Carrie Louise, Sept. 28, 1998

The early morning dance at 1421 Sylvan Street began before dawn, when Carrie would steal through the sleeping house to get a jump on the complicated choreography of waking up children and sending them off for their different schools and activities. It was the mid-1950s, and with children ranging in age from toddlers to teenagers, keeping their entire household on track required some military-style coordination and decades-old foresight.

"Rise and shine," she would whisper to Gwendolyn, shaking her daughter's shoulder. "You need to help me get everybody ready."

Gwendolyn, age ten, was her mother's lieutenant in the morning skirmish, and she knew by experience—no one had ever told her—that it would be full-time work for all hands to make ready six children neat and clean, fed and delivered to their respective schools.

When my twin Frederick and I were in kindergarten, we had our own special daily ritual. We went to the Lutheran kindergarten down on the other end of Sylvan Street when we were four and five. We were transported to this school by our family rather than by the community network that served the older children.

"Come on boys," Aunt Lizzie would say every morning, with the patient half-smile of someone who knew that getting five-year-old twins out the door was mostly about humor laced with a little bit of firmness. "Now, let's show your teacher how nicely Carrie's children sit in school."

The walk along Sylvan Street to the Lutheran kindergarten was short but emblematic, delivering both kinds of independence for us twins: our first taste of school-day freedom away from parents, yet still anchored to family oversight. Aunt Lizzie, who was taking her own independent course in nursing based on her sister Carrie's example, took this walking time as an opportunity for reinforcing in the children hard lessons about respect, responsibility, and representation in the community that should guide all our public behavior.

"You remember," she would call as we raced toward the kindergarten door, "you're more than Frederick and Clarence. You're Carrie's children, and everyone knows what that means. Act like it."

When we were dismissed around noon from kindergarten, our father Clarence Sr. was waiting, ready to walk us home, leading to a midday reunion that interrupted his workday and allowed him part of an afternoon with us boys while our older sisters remained at Saint Elizabeth and our mother at the clinic.

"How was school today?" he would ask them as they walked back home down Sylvan Street, eager to hear tales of kindergarten adventure and seizing the moment of their walk to drive home the educational values both parents emphasized.

"Today we learned letters," one twin might announce.

"We were singing songs about numbers," the other would say back.

It was these little conversations that allowed Clarence Sr. to keep tabs on his sons' educational progress while juggling his often sparse, often frustrating work obligations. The midday walks were amongst the best of times for father and sons to bond before the grinding reality of an opportunity in Cleveland would ultimately pull Clarence Sr. away because of economic necessity.

At 1421 Sylvan Street, Ms. Emma McCracken would be waiting to watch the twins after school. The neighbor's presence was essential for the delicate workings of the family's schedule. She made sure the boys ate lunch, stayed out of everyone's way outside, and were well watched over until the older children came home from Saint Elizabeth at 2:30 and Carrie from her clinic at about 4:30.

"Come on in, boys," Ms. Emma would say as we raced home and up the steps. As she welcomed us home from kindergarten, she'd announce, "I baked some tea cakes this morning, and we have milk to go with them."

Ms. Emma's care was much more than just babysitting—it was the embedded community scaffolding that made it possible for Carrie to continually operate as a professional while ensuring all of her children got the attention they needed and deserved. Next to our formal schooling, we twins learned from Ms. Emma's patient watchfulness.

But our educational journey began in earnest when we turned six years old and joined our older siblings on their daily trek to Saint Elizabeth Catholic School. For six children, the daily march was a parade neighbors could set their watches by and a reminder to everyone that this family pursued education with unyielding determination.

Saint Elizabeth Catholic School was unlike anything most of Selma's colored children would ever know. The single-story red brick rectangular building lay adjacent to the railroad tracks on its west. Being near the L&N line meant that classes were sometimes mildly interrupted, to the children's pleasure, by the rumble and whistle of freight trains carrying products from Selma's factories to markets throughout the South.

On the opposite side of the tracks, the school faced Knox Academy, where Carrie had received her own elementary education not too many years ago. Saint Elizabeth created a visual reminder of how much educational opportunities had expanded in a single generation, despite the "separate but equal" segregated school system in Alabama and states across the country. Often in early mornings before school or at recess, the students would engage in a friendly rock throwing across the tracks between the schools. These events symbolized schoolyard loyalty, for sure, but also the competitive drive that led all of us to treat our academic accomplishments as highly personal affairs.

The only variations in the predictable morning walks to Saint Elizabeth were the times when the children got an early start and could stop at the small candy factory on the corner of Small Avenue and Church Street. The shop, which was about a block away from school, enamored the children for its peanut brittle and pecan pralines. As they stepped in, visitors entered a world of oversized copper pots, clanging machines, and moving conveyors as candied pralines and chunks of peanut brittle were sorted in various directions. The kind store owner would sell the children a small brown bag filled with broken pieces of peanut brittle for ten cents. Since Carrie's family collected pecans from the three trees in their yard, the shop owner would buy their bagged pecans as well.

Inside Saint Elizabeth, everything coincided with the genuine educational mission taking place. The hallways, which stretched the full length of the building, were painted a distinctive creamy lime green, always smelling of fresh wax and chalk dust, institutional aromas that denoted real learning was happening. The classrooms were all the same in size and shape, with cinderblock walls painted in a cream-colored enamel that gave them a smooth, professional texture rivaling any other school in Alabama.

Within these classroom walls, the nuns—the Sisters of Saint Joseph—helped make Saint Elizabeth an incredible learning place. It was the simple truth that these women who were with the Catholic Mission had given their lives to ensure that these colored children obtained as refined an education as could be had in any place. They were not just teachers; they were great educators in the fullest sense of what an educator is. They put so much time and effort into developing skills, character, spirituality, culture, and confidence.

In the twenty-first century, many ugly truths have come to light about the Catholic Church and its educational institutions: excessive discipline, sometimes taking the form of physical abuse; sexual misconduct among the clergy; improper use of funds. Among the nuns and priests at Saint Elizabeth, however, none of these issues took shape in any way Carrie's children could see. The experiences they had in the school proved its teachers and administrators to be goodhearted people following the example of Christ.

Whereas the public schools for colored children were good enough, they tended to focus on rudimentary literacy, vocational training, and other practical affairs. Saint Elizabeth, on the other hand, provided a classical education that assumed every student was college bound and could, if given incentive, be intellectually excellent. The nuns cared nothing for the limits that a segregated society tried to impose on what their students could be.

Sister Francis Mary, who taught first and second grades, personified Saint Elizabeth's approach to education. She was beautiful and young, and she moved as someone who knew she was shaping the next generation of leaders. She loved and emphasized beautiful penmanship not for its own sake, but because she was fostering the idea that how we present ourselves in the world matters, and that perfection in small things leads to perfection in large ones.

"Your handwriting echoes your character," she would instruct her students while they practiced their letters in carefully drawn script. "So, immediately when someone sees your writing, they know they see a person who's proud of their work and values clarity of communication."

For a young boy like me, Sister Francis Mary was a new experience—a beautiful woman who was smart and dedicated to doing things for others. Although I was young, from what I knew of the life of nuns, I found her decision to become a nun strange. Her approach to teaching and focus on beautiful work, however, would influence me deeply.

Sister Francis Mary made me understand that beautiful work was not only possible; it was necessary in how you saw yourself. Not just acceptable work or good enough work, but absolutely beautiful work that would reflect the care and attention you brought to whatever you were doing.

As the children entered third and fourth grades, we would be welcomed by Sister Marie Helen, whose rosy cheeks and wire-rimmed glasses made her look like a kindly cherub, but indeed, she was a brilliant teacher. She had a special talent for making learning feel like playing (and we all know how hard that is), while ensuring serious academic progress.

Sister Marie Helen's love of reading made her know how to excite a classroom, to drop all self-consciousness and actively arouse curiosity and imagination. She loved reading out loud to children. She would position her third and fourth graders around her desk after lunch and transport them to other worlds through dramatic readings. She would do all these voices of the characters of a book, and her love for literature was infectious.

"Reading isn't just about recognizing words on a page," she would explain to her students. "Reading is an opening to traveling to places you've never been, meeting people you've never met, and sharing in experiences that broaden your view of the world and what's possible in life."

The daily reading sessions with Sister Marie Helen were memories to last a lifetime as well as seeds of reading habits to serve the students throughout their academic lives and beyond. They discovered that books were permanent fountains of education, exploration, and entertainment. Stories could impart lessons about life and imagination that were as valuable as factual knowledge.

The transition to fifth and sixth grades brought students under the guidance of Sister Marie Albert and later the wonderful Sister Josepha, who continued the tradition of combining academic rigor with cultural enrichment through storytelling. Sister Josepha's daily reading sessions were legendary. Her animated voice brought entire stories to life over weeks and months of after-lunch sessions.

I recall how she read the complete story of Peanuts by Charles Schulz, and the entire unabridged story of the Boxcar Children. She became each character, and we could see everything happening in our imaginations. When she described the grilled onions and boiled potatoes over an open log fire, the smell and taste were as good as in life. Those were among my most enjoyable years at Saint Elizabeth.

But Sister Josepha also demonstrated how faith and current events intersected in ways that made abstract concepts real and immediate.

When she asked her class to pray for her former classmate Roger Staubach to win in the Army–Navy football matchup of 1963, she was teaching students that prayer could be personal and specific, that the people you cared about mattered to God, and that faith was something you lived rather than just studied.

When news of President John F. Kennedy's assassination reached Selma, Sister Josepha's tears taught the children that adults could be vulnerable, that tragic events affected everyone regardless of their position or authority, and that grief was a natural response to loss that warranted community support and comfort.

The final years of Saint Elizabeth education came in seventh and eighth grades under the direct guidance of Sister Francis David, and later Sister Mary Paul, the principal. They both were stern but kindhearted, fair but demanding, and utterly committed to ensuring their graduates left Saint Elizabeth prepared for any academic challenge they might encounter.

"You should be prepared for any high school in the country by the time you leave," Sister Mary Paul would say to her eighth graders. More than that, you should understand that education is not something that happens to you—it's something you actively pursue throughout your entire life."

The daily routine at Saint Elizabeth was regimented in ways that taught discipline, respect, and the importance of order and preparation. Each school day worked like clockwork from 8:30 a.m. until 2:30 in the afternoon. The morning routine never varied: boys raising shades and opening windows, followed by the Pledge of Allegiance and a patriotic song that reinforced American ideals and democratic values.

The academic program was remarkably sophisticated for elementary school. The nuns would cover subjects like handwriting, spelling, music, and art with two grades simultaneously—first and second grades paired in one group, third and fourth grades in another, and so on—creating opportunities for peer learning and collaborative work. Then they would alternate between grades for subjects like English, history, geography, arithmetic, and science, giving assignments to one grade while providing direct instruction to the other.

This system required exceptional teaching skills and produced remarkable results. Students learned to work independently, when necessary, to support classmates who needed help, and to maintain focus and discipline even when their teacher's attention was directed elsewhere. They developed self-reliance, collaborative skills, and the kind of academic maturity that would serve them well in high school and beyond.

The curriculum included elements that most elementary schools couldn't provide, even among white schools. Visual and performing arts programs introduced students to classical music and art masters. Music appreciation classes broadened their cultural horizons. Science Research Associates (SRA) reading labs allowed advanced readers to progress at their own pace, ensuring that intellectual gifts were nurtured rather than constrained by grade-level limitations. Weekly spelling bees fostered honest competition, hard work, and top-notch spellers.

But the most transformative element of Saint Elizabeth education was the daily singing that occurred after lunch and second recess. The entire school would gather to sing Latin hymns, gospels, Black spirituals, and Irish folk songs—a musical program that celebrated both Catholic tradition and cultural diversity.

Throughout grade school I always enjoyed singing immensely. I knew I had a beautiful soprano voice, and sometimes when singing the Catholic hymns in Latin with the nuns, one of them would tell me I had such a lovely voice.

These communal singing sessions weren't just music education; they were daily affirmations of faith, culture, and community that connected students of diverse ages, creating memories for life. The combination of sacred and secular music, of disparate cultures' traditions, taught students that diversity could be a source of strength and beauty in different ways. And including music from the Black American cultural lineage showed the young colored students that their history was worth celebrating.

A daily singing schedule also featured geography songs, which aided in remembering the names of oceans, countries, seas, and continents. Students sang about multiplication tables and historical events. Musical repetition and catchy tunes were both entertaining and memorable, displaying that knowledge could be both serious and enjoyable, and that education should appeal to different senses and learning styles.

Years later, meeting people from across the country, Carrie's children could always identify others who had attended Catholic schools taught by nuns. There was something unmistakable about the formation they had received: the combination of academic rigor, cultural breadth, moral development, modest dressing, and unshakeable confidence that they could succeed in any environment.

The education had been so distinctive that it created an immediately recognizable type of person: someone who could think independently but work collaboratively, who understood that individual excellence meant nothing without collective advancement, and who brought both intellectual curiosity and practical skills to whatever challenges they faced.

But the education the Jones children received extended far beyond our formal classroom instruction at Saint Elizabeth. The community itself provided lessons in kindness, generosity, and the importance of caring relationships that crossed family lines. Perhaps no one embodied these lessons more completely than Mrs. Willie Mae Dawson, who lived on Small Avenue halfway between 1421 Sylvan Street and Hettie's house on Saint Ann Street.

Mrs. Willie Mae was a friend of Hettie's and a fellow member of Green Street Baptist Church, but she had carved out a special place in her heart for Frederick and me that went far beyond normal neighborly affection. She had a rarely seen adult son and a husband who worked as a Pullman porter with the Southern Railway Company, traveling routes that kept him away from home for weeks at a time. In the absence of daily family companionship, she had fondly adopted us twins as her favorite little boys, keeping us stuffed with cakes, muffins, and pies whenever we appeared at her door.

Mrs. Willie Mae's small house was a wonderland for children, filled with the sort of small moving trinkets and bobbing heads of turtles and donkeys that could fascinate any young visitor for hours. But it was her kitchen that truly captured our devotion. Mrs. Willie Mae made what were easily the best muffins and pound cakes in the neighborhood, using what I suspected were vanilla and almond extracts as her secret ingredients—flavors I would experiment with years later when I learned to cook and bake for myself.

The sweetness extended beyond her baking to her generous sharing of the three apricot trees that graced her backyard. When the fruit ripened each summer, she would invite us to pick freely from the branches, loading them down with more apricots than two boys could eat. The surplus always found its way to Carrie, who would transform the fruit into jams and preserves during the communal canning sessions that brought neighbors together in mutual support and shared abundance.

But Mrs. Willie Mae's most distinctive characteristic was her enthusiastic love of baseball. Watching games was her favorite pastime, and she had strong opinions about her favorite players: Willie Mays, Mickey Mantle, and Hank Aaron topped her list of heroes whose exploits she followed with the dedication of a professional scout. She would invite Frederick and me to watch games with her, providing running commentary about strategy, player statistics, and the finer points of the sport that helped us develop our own appreciation for America's pastime.

This love of baseball led to what would become one of the most memorable gifts either of us would ever receive. Mrs. Willie Mae had learned that she could collect S&H Green Stamps from her grocery shopping at the A&P Store. Rather than redeeming them for household items she didn't need, she began giving her stamp books to Frederick and me. Throughout each year, she would always hand over every green stamp she received, helping us paste them into the collection books that we would eventually redeem for something special.

"Y'all save these all year," she would tell us as she handed over another sheet of the small green squares that represented her grocery purchases, "and when Christmas comes around, you'll have enough to get yourselves something really nice."

By the end of the next year, the accumulated stamps were enough to redeem for genuine official-size leather baseball gloves, not the cheap substitutions that most children had to settle for, but real equipment that any serious young ball player would be proud to own. The annual trip to the redemption center was a highlight we looked forward to all year round and the baseball gloves we received were treasures that connected us not only to the sport we loved but to the woman whose thoughtfulness had made the gifts possible.

Mrs. Willie Mae's influence on us twins extended far beyond the items she offered us or the treats and baked goods she spoiled us with. She displayed the kind of purposeful kindness that could convert casual connections into bonds that existed independently of biology. She demonstrated to us that love could be conveyed through minor gestures such as remembering our preferred flavors of ice cream, sensing when we needed encouragement and delivering it, and pausing to explain things we didn't quite understand.

Most significantly, she taught us that community assistance could come from surprising sources. While Carrie was giving medical care for families throughout Selma, Mrs. Willie Mae was giving emotional care to two small boys who needed to realize that they were crucial to someone outside of their nuclear family. Her house was a distinct kind of sanctuary where we knew we would indeed discover warmth, meals, entertainment, and the type of unconditional acceptance that instilled confidence in our inherent value.

The kinship with Mrs. Willie Mae also revealed just how the support system of Carrie's children extended from the community in ways not always visible but always reliable. When their neighbors saw the twins walking to or from Mrs. Willie Mae's house, they knew there was more to it than some kids visiting an elderly woman on a regular basis. They were watching their community take ownership over raising its young, making sure no child was left without the kind of personal attention and loving care that would enable them to flourish.

Later in life, when Frederick and I had moved to Atlanta, grew up, and made our lives there among other adult citizens of the city, we would often look back on Mrs. Willie Mae's house as a place where we had been privileged to learn some valuable lessons about generosity, consideration for what others might need from you, and how kindness could create lasting ties between individuals who decided that they would care out of choice. The baseball gloves had deteriorated long ago, but the belief that a community of people could provide not just for a child's happiness, but also development as an individual—that was something embedded deeply within us.

Mrs. Willie Mae would live on in our hearts forever, not merely as the lady who'd handed out S&H Green Stamps and the best muffins in Selma, but who had taught us that love was found in so many little acts it added up to something great. Her legacy survived in our own willingness to see when others needed kindness and that a community was created one relationship at a time, by choosing intentionally to care for people who may have otherwise gone unnoticed.

The Jones children's learning continued beyond the classroom and the homes of neighbors, extending into the four walls of our own home. The kitchen at 1421 Sylvan Street was Carrie's second schoolroom, where she taught lessons about sustenance and preparation and the alchemy of turning ordinary ingredients into expressions of love and care. Carrie, like her mother Hettie before her, was a great cook who knew that food was not just fuel—it was comfort, party, and education all in one.

The pantry wasn't always full, and was sometimes nearly bare, but that never stopped Carrie from quickly cooking up something sweet or soothing to eat at breakfast. Grits and eggs were the mainstay of breakfast, a practical and filling meal that fed children who had to last until late afternoon for lunch at school. But sometimes, particularly on her days off or when she felt the family could use extra comfort, she would make one of two breakfast dishes that the children regarded as special.

The baked cinnamon rice and raisin pudding filled the kitchen with sweeping scents that proclaimed love before anyone saw the dish. The smell of cinnamon, fused with the sweetness of raisins and creaminess born from baked rice, provided olfactory welcome that could make even the coldest morning feel warm and full of promise. The children's other favorite was her baked rice and cheese, savory rather than sweet, but comfort food just the same.

None of these recipes were fancy or involved costly ingredients; they were simple things treated with attention and care. They showed the children that food could be nourishing in a practical sense and pleasurable as well, that scarcity did not mean the end of joy and culinary creativity, and that mealtimes were when love could be tasted in well-seasoned dishes prepared with consideration of what would bring comfort or delight.

On Sundays, and on her days off from the clinic, Carrie would also take some time to show one child or another how to cook at least one or two dishes or bake a cake. These weren't just what-I'm-making-anyway demonstrations: Mommie would give a lesson that involved math, measurement, timing, technique, and mindfulness, the things that turned just cooking into *cooking* for great cooks.

"You have to measure the sugar and flour just right," she'd say as she demonstrated how to level measuring cups and measuring spoons. "Baking is more science than art. If you don't get the proportions right, nothing after that will do the trick."

She'd demonstrate how to beat the batter so it felt just right, how the texture would be just so, so when they made it themselves after that, they'd know when to get the cake into the oven. They'd learn how to crack eggs without getting shards in the bowl, how to tell if butter was softened but not melted, and how to recognize that baking required the same kind of concentration and care that schoolwork demands.

For the twins, Frederick and me, upside-down pineapple cake would be the first cake we learned to make—a recipe that combined following precise instructions with the dramatic reveal when you inverted the pan and discovered whether your caramelized pineapple topping had worked or not. Later we would learn to make banana pudding, mastering the art of creating proper custard and layering ingredients for maximum effect.

Years later in college, I would make my own version: a frozen banana pudding that became famous among roommates and friends. Whenever someone needed comfort or celebration, I'd prepare the dish Mommie had first taught me to make, discovering that the recipe carried not just flavor but the memory of her patient instruction and the understanding that feeding people was a form of care.

It is fair to add that the teaching occurred not ultimately through a single recipe but through a series of recipes and other lessons on food preparation and kitchen management. The children learned to read the recipe carefully, not to skip steps or add the wrong ingredients, to organize themselves to have all the ingredients at hand before starting, to clean up as they were cooking and not at the end of the disaster, to validate with a taste and adjust the seasoning rather than rely upon the accuracy of the instructions.

One late afternoon when Carrie came back from work, Gwendolyn, who was ten or eleven at the time, had produced biscuits for the first time on her own without any help or supervision. They were not a total success, although not a complete failure. She didn't recall putting in the baking powder, so instead of puffed fluffiness her biscuits were thin and flat. But Carrie's reaction became a lesson that Gwendolyn would remember for the rest of her life.

Carrie didn't criticize or express disappointment. Rather, she hugged her daughter and threw her in the air and squeezed her tightly while smiling as broadly as the sky. She ran to the pan of jumbled biscuits and out to the front porch, calling across the street to Mrs. Ethel Parnell.

"Mrs. Ethel! Come to your porch! I want to tell you something!" she shouted with unmistakable joy in her voice. When Mrs. Ethel stepped out, Carrie announced proudly that her Gwen had made her first pan of biscuits, all by herself; no one had helped her! The absence of baking powder was a mere half-truth, a sidenote to the greater accomplishment of independence and achievement.

"You made them all by yourself," Carrie repeated to Gwendolyn a few minutes later. "You won't forget the powder again, but more importantly, now you know! That's how you learn, sweetheart. You don't come out born knowing, you learn. And you do it by trying, by trying over and over again."

Carrie's approach to teaching never made errors matters of tears or fear; errors were matters of course. Practicing made perfect sense, and errors made knowledge of what not to do; her pride was not based on perfection but initiative.

Summer brought different types of food lessons. For starters, with the weather warm and the kids off from school, barbecues became regular social affairs, with the frequent presence of others in the home and backyard. It quickly became clear that Uncle John's housewarming gift of a barbecue pit had been for the neighborhood as much as for the family.

Carrie would prepare her chickens the spatchcock way, by splitting the bird and flattening the pieces for even grilling. She and Uncle John had developed their own special sauce—ketchup-based but elevated with vinegar, sugar or honey, a little lemon juice, and black pepper. The secret, they instructed the kids who were paying attention, was to bring the sauce to a simmer before applying it as a basting to the chicken. This cooking step turned the raw taste of vinegar into something mellow and helped forge the flavors together in a way that brushing on cold sauce could never accomplish. Before the chicken went on the grill, it would be plunged briefly into simmering vinegar seasoned with salt and pepper, a preparation that would become part of my own method of grilling years later as I matured into what my family came to call a grill master.

Savory smells of simmering sauce and roasting chicken would waft down the block, beckoning neighbors to gather in the backyard where they knew there'd be good food, camaraderie, and the sort of open-armed hospitality that Carrie's family was known for. Nobody who showed up was turned away; there was always enough to go around and a seat at a table or space to stand around the grill. Uncle John always made sure there was plenty of everything, both food and drinks: dozens of chickens and a tub full of iced Carling Black Label, Schlitz, and his favorite Budweiser. And Uncle DeeDee was there, regaling the kids with tall tales and cracking jokes.

Birthday celebrations, no matter how modest, were never skipped or minimized. Carrie would prepare parties for each child, inviting a few friends, playmates, and cousins. At minimum there would always be homemade cake and sometimes homemade ice cream, created with the hand-crank ice cream maker that required everyone taking turns at the tedious work of churning.

These celebrations were not about lavish gifts or expensive happenings. They were about commemorating each child's separate significance, so that every birthday boy or girl felt noticed and important on his or her special day. The subliminal message was, "You matter; your life is worthy of celebration, and within this family we respect the conscience of each person's life with attentiveness and labor."

The big Catholic holy days brought even more elaborate preparations. Carrie always remained Baptist like her mother Hettie before her, but when each of her children chose to take up the Catholic faith of their schooling with personal conviction, she supported their decision. When children had their Baptism or Confirmation, the dining table would be set beautifully with linens and adorned like a king's banquet: platters of candied yams, macaroni and cheese, collard greens, and whatever meat the budget allowed. Everyone would be dressed in their Sunday best for these occasions, understanding that marking important religious milestones required the same kind of attention and ceremony that the church itself provided.

For the Christmas and Easter holidays, the table itself would once again be the closest thing to elegance achievable, proof that celebration did not require wealth so much as it necessitated attention to detail—and commitment to proper recognition and commemoration under the auspices of the dignity and joy in the room.

Life lessons abounded at home and in the community, but Saint Elizabeth remained central to the children's intellectual and spiritual formation, even when they left the schoolhouse. The walk home from Saint Elizabeth each afternoon was as important as the walk to school each morning. The children would often stop at Ben's Barbecue Cafe, where they could buy cookies and candy while dancing to music from the jukebox. These stops weren't just about the treats; they were opportunities to practice social skills, to interact with classmates and other children, and to decompress from the intensive academic work they'd completed during the day.

"Don't spend too long dancing," Carolyn would warn her younger siblings as they lingered at Ben's jukebox. "Mommie expects us home by three o'clock, and we still have homework to do."

The homework sessions at 1421 Sylvan Street were as regimented as the school day itself. The large dining room table became command central for academic work, with older children helping younger ones while Carrie supervised when she wasn't away for medical emergencies.

They all knew the household rule: "Everyone helps everyone younger than them." This rule governed both homework and everything else. If you understand something that someone else is struggling with, you help them understand it too.

This approach to learning extended far beyond formal academics. The children learned that knowledge was meant to be shared, that personal success was meaningless without collective advancement, and that education was both privilege and responsibility.

By the time a student finished the eighth grade, they were well on a solid path to a college education. The foundation was that strong; the preparation that thorough.

But perhaps even more important was how the Saint Elizabeth experience helped shape the children's own understandings of their capacities and place in the world. They were taught that intelligence was something to be nurtured and used for the benefit of others. They knew that they could tackle anything academic. They knew that excellence was not only achievable but expected.

They had a warm memory of those days—how the community acknowledged and praised their educational achievement. Whenever all six children walked to school together, covering the six to eight blocks from Sylvan Street to Church Street, friends and neighbors would call out, "There goes Carrie's kids!"

The phrase carried layers of meaning that the children internalized without fully understanding. Recognition of their mother's reputation and the respect she had earned through her service to the community. Pride in the educational opportunity they were receiving through Dr. Dumont's charity. Acknowledgment that these children were being prepared for futures that would extend far beyond Selma's city limits.

"There goes Carrie's kids" also expressed expectations. The

community knew that these children were receiving opportunities most colored kids couldn't get, and those openings came with responsibilities. Carrie's kids were supposed to study hard, act with honor and respect, and use their education in a way not to serve themselves but to serve the community at large.

The children felt the pressure of those expectations, but they also felt elevated by them. And they knew that their success mattered to many more people than just members of their family and that the education they had received offered broader possibilities for other children who might follow them.

When the family moved to Atlanta in summer 1967, after the first six children had completed their elementary education at Saint Elizabeth, they carried with them more than academic preparation. They carried confidence from knowing they could succeed in any educational environment, understanding that learning was a lifelong pursuit, and conviction that their knowledge should be used in service of others.

The sisters of Saint Elizabeth had given them something precious—not just a good education but a solid confidence in their own capacity to think and the knowledge that they must use that thinking wisely. The bedrock had been set, and now the world would learn what "There goes Carrie's kids" actually meant as these kids went about changing America.

CHAPTER EIGHT

The Sacred and the Movement

The stained-glass windows of Saint Elizabeth Catholic Church had always captivated me, the way morning light came through in patterns of red, blue, and gold that progressed across the wooden pews as the sun moved higher. For me and Frederick, the church had become as familiar as our own home—a place where we learned discipline, reverence, and the kind of quiet trust that came from having important obligations.

From the time we were small enough to kneel beside our mother on the occasional Sundays she attended Mass— either in addition to or instead of the service at Green Street Baptist—both of us watched the altar boys, many of whom were our cousins, with something close to envy. The white surplices over red cassocks looked dignified and important, and the way the boys moved through their duties with practiced strictness made serving at the altar seem like the most natural thing in the world.

When Brother Edmund eventually asked us to join the altar boy training, both of us recognized we were entering something meaningful, not just to the church but to our own growth as young men who could be given serious duties.

"Clarence, you'll be at the 6:30 morning Mass at the Convent," Brother Edmund declared at one of our Saturday meetings. "The Sisters specifically requested you." Frederick would stick with the service for the larger Sunday congregations and other special feast days, assignments that required their own kind of skill and care.

At ten years old, serving daily Mass at the Sisters of Saint Joseph Convent was quite a difficult responsibility. It meant rising before dawn and walking through Selma's quiet streets while most people were still sleeping, just like our mother did for early morning birthing calls. The assignment did have its small rewards, however. I would share breakfast each morning with the nuns—meaning one less mouth for Mommie to feed at home—and daily practice with Latin responses that would make me the most proficient altar boy at Saint Elizabeth.

The 5:45 a.m. walk each morning to the Convent on Broad Street wasn't easy at first, but it became as routine as breathing. Sylvan Street belonged to shift workers heading to the factories, neighbors starting their day, and on Small Avenue, delivery trucks rumbling toward downtown. The air carried familiar scents: wood smoke from breakfast fires, yeast from the bakery beginning its daily production, and an occasional sweet smell of peppermint from the candy factory.

Inside the Convent chapel, everything felt different from regular Sunday Mass. It was quieter and more intimate, the atmosphere evoking the concentrated devotion of women who had dedicated their lives to prayer and service. The Sisters filed in wearing their habits, faces peaceful in the way that came from starting each day in communion with God.

"*Introibo ad altare Dei*," Father McNiece would start, and I would answer with the Latin that by now I knew as well as English: "*Ad Deum qui laetificat juventutem meam*."

The entire Mass was in Latin, an effect that created the feeling of ancient ritual and universal tradition linking this small chapel in Selma, Alabama to Catholic churches around the world. As a young boy coming of age in the segregated South, these daily Masses taught me a powerful lesson about universality: Faith cannot be confined by the artificial lines through which we divide ourselves in secular society.

Nor can devotion to God be split along arbitrary racial lines as it seemed to be in churches all across America.

After Mass, breakfast with the nuns proved to be an experience that informed my understanding of religious life and dedication. The Sisters would have me at their morning meal as if I were one of them, inquiring about my studies, my family, and what I thought of the readings we had just heard.

"You have a lovely voice for the responses," Sister Josepha would say to me over oatmeal and fruit. "You ever think about what you would like to be when you grow up?"

"I don't know yet, Sister. Something that helps people, like my mother does."

"That's a strong base for any decision you make in life," she'd say. "Remember that God gives us gifts so that we can help others with them."

These talks laid the groundwork in ways that went way beyond religious orientation. The nuns treated me like an intelligent young person who had the potential to think seriously and contribute something real, and not merely as a child to be managed. They fostered my curiosity, valued my opinions, and showed through their own lives what it meant to serve.

But the most deep-seated element of my altar boy experience was learning how to straddle worlds that existed within my daily life: the sacred world of Latin Masses and religious ritual, and the increasingly active world of civil rights organizing that was just starting to galvanize Selma's colored community.

By ten years old, I was attending civil rights mass meetings with the same regularity as the daily Masses I served in the Convent. Both activities were about faith, but they came in dramatically different forms—one expressed through ancient liturgy and contemplative prayer, the other through freedom songs and collective action aimed at changing unjust social systems.

My first mass meeting had been pure coincidence, the result of childhood curiosity rather than planned involvement. Walking along Broad Street after serving a late evening Mass, I noticed something unusual: white men with rifles sitting in cars parked along the street. The unusual sight drew me toward the building these men were casing: Tabernacle Baptist Church. Inside I discovered a gathering unlike anything I had experienced before.

There was something electric about the atmosphere inside Tabernacle Baptist, in a way that was entirely different from Catholic liturgy yet powerful in its own right. Where the Convent chapel was hushed and contemplative, the mass meeting vibrated with energy, hopefulness, and the sort of collective resolve that made personal fear feel bearable.

"We're going to keep meeting until all of us can register to vote," the speaker was saying as I sat down toward the back of the church. "We're going to continue organizing until our children can attend any school that they qualify for. We're going to keep marching until justice gets served in this city."

The words touched something deep in my own understanding of what faith expected. The daily Masses at the Convent demonstrated to me that God demanded service to others, that private salvation was nothing without collective redemption, that faith without works was empty ceremony. The mass meetings were putting those very principles of love into practice, only in the social and political realm rather than the purely spiritual. This may have been one of the first mass meetings to take place in Selma during this period, making me an accidental witness to the beginning of organized resistance that would eventually transform not just our city but the entire country.

The singing at mass meetings was different from the Latin hymns I sang among the nuns, but it had a similar transformative power to integrate individual voices into something greater than their sum. When Reverend Hosea Williams led the congregation in hymn singing, the voices that joined together created the same sense of transcendence that I experienced during the most solemn moments of Catholic liturgy.

Just being there and singing, you could see the spirits of a whole congregation become one and be carried to levels you've never been before. You could hear and see tears of joy intermingle with those of sadness as many voices became one voice, a voice steeped in bravery and bounded by the warm embrace of readiness.

This was my first taste of a realization that faith could be both contemplative and active, personal and political, ancient but urgently contemporary. The altar boy training that gave me discipline, responsibility, and a mentality not to take sacred concepts lightly was also nurturing me for involvement in a movement that would demand those same virtues of personal responsibility—this time in the service of social justice.

As altar boys, one form of education and community that Frederick and I received was through the weekly altar boy meetings on Saturdays. The mission of Brother Edmund and Father McNiece was to organize Masses, collect cassocks, see that the altar boys knew their Latin responses, and provide an early education for young boys who would be future candidates for the priesthood.

But the altar boy program was about more than religious formation or preparation for vocational service to the church. The weekly meetings included movies, trips to Dairy Queen for ice cream and Brazier burgers, and overnight camping trips to a campground called Joyland that exposed the boys to experiences beyond Selma's city limits. The early 1960s VW van that provided transportation for these adventures became a symbol of possibility—proof that the world was much bigger than what we could see from our Selma neighborhood.

The trip to Mobile, Alabama, where we boarded the docked USS Alabama battleship, was especially memorable. For young boys who had never been farther than fifty miles from home, walking through the massive warship was like entering another world entirely. We explored the gun turrets, sleeping quarters, and engine rooms, all while learning about the ship's role in World War II.

"This ship fought to win the war that gave us the opportunities we have today," Father McNiece said, standing on one of its decks as we watched Mobile Bay. "The men who served on this ship that we honor were fighting for freedom, just like the people in your community are fighting for freedom today."

For young boys growing up in the segregated South, these trips offered important perspective. We altar boys discovered that the world was more complicated, the universe larger than what we saw day to day; history was still being written, and we had a part in writing it.

The leaders of the Catholic community instituted a system of points for the altar boys. Each Mass served and each correctly recited Latin response earned an altar boy points he could use to purchase coupons, the same coupons that would be accepted by vendors of various items at Saint Elizabeth's annual Fall Festival & Bazaar. This arrangement taught us at an early age about the rewards to be had through faithful service.

I had a double advantage in accumulating points since I served daily Mass at the Convent and that daily service resulted in me getting more practice in memorizing the Latin responses. Throughout each year, I was able to gain enough points to purchase several grab bags at the Fall Festival, which always contained items that became Christmas gifts for my siblings.

I don't understand it, even today. I genuinely enjoy giving but have mixed feelings about receiving gifts. It's like not really knowing how to be happy on occasions where I should be. This pattern of finding more joy in giving than receiving was being forged in me through the altar boy program but reinforced by everything I observed at home. Carrie's continuous service to others, the family's practice of sharing whatever they had with neighbors who needed help, the understanding that individual prosperity meant nothing if the community was struggling—all of these influences were shaping a young person who would find satisfaction in contributing to something larger than himself.

The formation that I was receiving through my daily service at the Convent and my education at Saint Elizabeth would be tested in ways both small and important as I grew older. One of the most memorable tests came not during a dramatic moment but in the ordinary course of running errands with my twin brother after school.

On Broad Street, there was a small bakery that sold packages of sliced bread loaves—Holsum, Colonial and Merita—in addition to other baked goods like cakes, pies, and sweets like apple and peach turnovers and rectangular slices of pound cake. The warm, sweet smell that always surrounded the bakery made it next to impossible to go past without catching a whiff that hinted at comfort and contentment.

The shop was located directly across the street from Dr. Dumont's clinic, at the perpendicular crossing of Small Avenue and Broad. Both locations were down the street from Saint Elizabeth Church and a couple of blocks away from Saint Elizabeth Catholic School, making the bakery a natural stop for the children from either of the two routes they normally walked home from school.

On days after Carrie had been paid, Frederick and I would be regularly tasked with stopping by the bakery to purchase bread for the family. At ten cents per loaf, we would buy twenty loaves and place them in a large bag before taking it to the counter to pay. The Jewish shop owner, who knew our routine, had come to know us the same way the rest of the neighborhood did, as "Carrie's kids," the sons of the woman who worked across the street with Dr. Dumont.

On one memorable day, which would stay with me for the rest of my life, we followed our usual routine of selecting bread loaves, but on this occasion, we dropped two apple turnovers into the bottom before placing the bread in our bag. The decision wasn't forethought or discussed; it was the kind of impetuous choice that children sometimes make without fully weighing the consequences.

As we approached the counter with our bag, something unusual happened. The shop owner, who normally simply counted the loaves and accepted payment, started to reach into our bag, something he had never done before, since he knew the routine and how many loaves we typically purchased.

Our hearts started racing. We knew with certainty what the shopkeeper was about to discover. As the shop owner extracted the two apple turnovers from the bag, the silence in the small store felt overwhelming.

When he spoke, his voice was quiet but firm. "I know your mother would be very disappointed in you boys if she knew what you had done." He paused, looking directly at both of us with an expression of disappointment rather than anger. "You must promise to never do this again, here or anywhere, and I will not mention this to your mother."

Shakily, we said we were sorry and promised to never steal anything again. We paid for our bread and left the store, but the effect of the moment lingered with us long after we reached home. The shop owner's decision to handle what happened with grace rather than punishment, to appeal to our better nature rather than simply calling for punishment, made a deeper impression than any harsh response could have achieved.

This incident had a huge impact on me as I came of age morally. I would never again try to take anything that did not belong to me or that I didn't pay for. I never forgot that day and the shame of my action.

It wasn't a sense of being caught that shamed me. It was letting down someone who'd shown me kindness and respect, and breaking the trust I knew had been placed in me as one of Carrie's kids. The shopkeeper had recognized us, had known our mother's reputation in the local area, and because of who we were related to, had expected we would be better behaved.

The incident also reinforced lessons that were being taught simultaneously at home, at school, and at church about honor, honesty, and personal integrity. It was not only the healthy dose of Catholic guilt; I knew right from wrong and honor from dishonor not just from my Catholic upbringing but from Carrie's training—training I would never want to dishonor.

It was these three influences—the moral teachings of the Catholic church, my family ethos, and community expectations—which provided a moral compass for me for much of my life. I knew that what I did was not simply a reflection on myself but on my family, my school, and my faith community. Both privilege and obligation came with being labeled one of "Carrie's kids."

But the most transformative moment in my religious education came on a Sunday morning that would be remembered by everyone present. Father Maurice Ouellet, the new pastor from Canada, was offering the 10 a.m. Mass when he made an announcement that surprised everyone in the congregation, including all the Jones children.

"This morning," Father Ouellet said quietly, "we will all be walking to Our Lady Queen of Peace for Mass."

The silence that followed was profound. Our Lady Queen of Peace was the Catholic church attended by whites only. All across the United States, churches and parishes tended to manifest the segregated reality in other public spheres. Racially blended congregations were quite rare, especially in southern cities like Selma. Sometimes colored people were excluded from white congregations by subtle unwelcoming attitudes; other times colored people were allowed in the building but required to sit in specific, usually less favorable areas of the church. Often the exclusion was explicit, rude, and forceful, displaying in every way a lack of Christlike character.

The idea of Saint Elizabeth's entire colored congregation simply walking over to Our Lady Queen of Peace for Mass was unheard of. Yet churches were not only sites of racial division rearing its ugly head. Churches like Tabernacle Baptist, Brown Chapel, and First Baptist were incubators for resistance against racial oppression. Faith in God was an inspiration for countless civil rights leaders to pursue equity and justice. And Father Ouellet's calm authority made it clear that this wasn't a request; it was what was going to happen.

Parishioners filled the pews of Saint Elizabeth from front to back, casting furtive glances at one another before standing to follow their pastor out of that sanctuary and into the morning sun of Selma. What had been a twenty-minute walk to Our Lady Queen of Peace became a quiet procession of resolve, families walking side by side toward an act of integration, not one we had planned or wanted, but one we all were willing to try.

As undoubtedly expected, white parishioners at Our Lady Queen of Peace didn't receive us. No seats were offered. No usher extended a hand. The Saint Elizabeth parishioners were suspended in this open space near the rear of the sanctuary and spilling back out onto the church steps, attending Mass but clearly not invited to sit in these pews reserved for white Catholics.

The lack of welcome did not deter the children of God from Saint Elizabeth. We remained through the Mass as a silent protest of presence. It was my sibling's and my first taste of liturgical defiance, in which faith opposed injustice not with shouting, but in words of solemnity and sacrifice.

For me, this experience synthesized everything I had been learning as an altar boy and hearing while sitting in on meetings with civil rights leaders. Faith meant action, justice was valuable even when it hurt people's feelings, and Catholic principles learned in Latin class translated directly to the real-life outrages I saw every day in segregated Selma.

"Did Jesus ever say that some people couldn't sit in a place because of the color of their skin?" I asked Father McNiece later that week.

"No, son, he did not. That's why we went to Queen of Peace—to remind everyone that God's house should be open to all God's children."

This object lesson in applied Christianity would be crucial in the months and years ahead, when my siblings and I took part in actions that defied segregation outright. And the altar boy training that instilled in me a reverence for sacred things also taught me that some requirements—of human dignity, of equal treatment—were so sacred as to demand courageous action on their behalf.

Father Ouellet would later accompany the civil rights marchers on various occasions, led by Reverend F. D. Reese, to the Selma Courthouse with the goal of registering to vote. They would be stopped, as usual, by Sheriff Jim Clark and Public Safety Director Wilson Baker, but the presence of white clergy in the movement demonstrated the kind of moral authority that transcended racial boundaries. These same acts of courageous consciousness would lead to Archbishop Toolen asking Father Ouellet to leave Selma.

For the altar boys who witnessed this integration of faith and social action, the lessons were clear: Religious commitment meant more than believing the Bible, attending services, and learning prayers. It meant standing up for justice even when doing so required courage and sacrifice.

As I would later reflect, my time as an altar boy shaped my sense of service and leadership. The early mornings taught me the importance of punctuality. The Latin Mass taught me discipline. The nuns taught me respect. And the small church on Sylvan Street showed me how to hold my head high even when the world refused to let me.

These were the unspoken gifts Carrie also bequeathed by sending her sons out into the world with the tools to carry and construct themselves. She not only freed us; she gave us faith. Not only rules but reverence.

The sacred and the movement were not separate realms but different expressions of the same fundamental commitment to human dignity and divine justice. The Latin responses that I recited each morning were prayers for a world where all people could worship together, learn together, and live together as equals.

I would soon, very soon, learn that those prayers were being answered through the actions of ordinary people who managed to find extraordinary courage to stand up against injustice wherever they might meet it. The altar boy training that taught me discipline, reverence, and service was also preparing me to serve in ways that would help transform American society.

The groundwork had been laid—spiritual formation and social awareness working in tandem to create a generation of young people who knew that faith demanded action, service required sacrifice, and holy moments were generated whenever people joined forces in the righteous fight for a more just and loving world.

CHAPTER NINE

The March Begins in Selma

By the summer of 1964, the mass meetings at Brown Chapel, First Baptist, and Tabernacle Baptist had evolved from occasional gatherings into a regular rhythm of organizing, planning, and preparation. What had begun as conversations about voter registration and equal treatment had grown into something larger and more coordinated, a systematic challenge to the segregated order that had governed Selma for generations.

I, along with Joan, Yolanda, and our cousins Tena and Elaine, had become regular attendees at these meetings, no longer curious observers but devoted participants who understood that they were part of something special happening in Selma—maybe something historic. We had found our place in the movement not as symbolic figures but as sincere participants whose presence and energy helped sustain the adults who were taking the greatest risks.

"You young people give us hope," Reverend Hosea Williams of Tabernacle Baptist would tell us. "When we see you here, willing to be part of this fight, we know that what we're fighting for collectively is going to outlast any of us individually."

The civil rights activities that drew the children to mass meetings and marches weren't abstract protests of distant injustices. Instead, they were responses to the daily reality of segregation that shaped every aspect of life in Selma. Downtown Selma appeared prosperous and thriving, with several department stores, two movie theaters, two major bus lines, restaurants, and shops that suggested a community enjoying economic success. But for Black residents, this apparent prosperity came with constant reminders of their second-class status.

The posted signs saying *White Only* or *No Coloreds* were everywhere, marking water fountains, restrooms, lunch counters, and waiting areas with the blunt efficiency of legal segregation. These weren't subtle suggestions or informal customs. They were explicit declarations that certain spaces, services, and opportunities were off limits to citizens based solely on the color of their skin.

For a curious boy like me, these restrictions created a strange geography of access and exclusion that I navigated with the mixture of resentment and fascination that characterized many children's responses to illogical adult rules. When I was downtown, I would sometimes drop into the Greyhound bus station just to look around, I studied the signs showing which cities people were traveling to and from, and sat near the windows to watch the incoming and outgoing buses that connected Selma to the wider world.

The bus station carried the dense smell of diesel fuel that seemed to promise adventure and possibility, but even there the reality of segregation was inescapable. Separate waiting areas, separate ticket windows, separate restrooms—all maintained with the kind of institutional efficiency that made discrimination feel normal and permanent to those who had never known anything different.

Selma's movie theaters provided the most obviously absurd example of segregation's irrational premises. Signs directed Black patrons to go upstairs to the balcony while white patrons walked straight into their seating on the lower level. To my practical mind, this arrangement seemed backwards. The upper level clearly offered a better view of the movie screen, making the privilege of lower-level seating seem more like a disadvantage.

But regardless of the seating, the wafting aroma of popcorn and peanuts that permeated both levels served as a reminder that some experiences transcended racial boundaries even when the spaces themselves were artificially divided. The same movies, the same snacks, and the same human desire for entertainment and escape were all made meaningless by laws that insisted on separation where no natural barrier existed.

Reverend Williams had a powerful ability to motivate young people. His presence at the meetings, which resonated through his inspiring and empathetic voice, created an atmosphere of real possibility that made even the most dangerous plans seem plausible. He was joined by John Lewis, Reverend James Bevel, and Reverend Richard Boone to form a team that embodied the type of leadership that could channel the energy and idealism of young children and teenagers into effective social action.

The Easter-Wear Boycott that Reverend James Bevel organized in 1963 demonstrated how the movement could change even the most traditional celebrations into statements of social conscience and economic resistance. Bevel had already gained notoriety for his work with the Southern Christian Leadership Conference, his partnerships with civil rights leaders like Dr. Martin Luther King Jr., and his involvement in momentous projects like the Birmingham Children's Crusade, which mobilized young students as well as adults. The Easter-Wear Boycott went beyond symbolism; it was a coordinated effort to show that dignity didn't depend on material possessions and that the community could unite around shared values rather than individual display.

"We're going to show that our worth doesn't come from what we can afford to buy or wear," Reverend Bevel announced at the mass meeting where the boycott was planned. "Every family that participates will be making a testimony that our success is based on character, not on clothes."

For weeks before Easter, the message was emphasized at mass meetings and through the network of churches and community organizations. Instead of new Easter outfits, everyone would wear what Reverend Bevel wore consistently; white shirts and denim overalls, with combat boots if you had them.

At 1421 Sylvan Street, this meant quite a different Easter preparation than the children had previously experienced. Instead of Carrie working late into the night on her Singer sewing machine to create new Easter outfits for nine children, she explained why this Easter would be different and what the family's participation would demonstrate.

"How do we look?" the children asked as we prepared for Easter Sunday service, each dressed in simple work clothes.

"You look like children who understand that some things are more important than appearances," Carrie replied. "You look like young people who are willing to sacrifice for principles they believe in."

By the time I was ten years old, I had already become one of what would later be called the eager young civil rights foot soldiers. For me, my sisters Yolanda and Joan, my cousins Tena and Elaine, and countless other children throughout Selma, attending mass meetings, sit-ins, and marches had become as natural as going to school or church. These were activities that combined social interaction with education in ways that would shape our understanding of citizenship and moral responsibility for the rest of our lives.

The churches where meetings regularly took place were within easy walking distance of most children's homes. Brown Chapel AME and First Baptist Church were both on Sylvan Street, just three or four blocks from the Jones family's home at 1421 Sylvan Street. Tabernacle Baptist Church, on Broad Street, was only three doors down from Saint Elizabeth Catholic Church, making it simple for children to move between our formal education and our political education without requiring special transportation or parental coordination.

During the summer months especially, there was always activity at these churches, and never a day without warm scents greeting anyone who entered. The coffee brewing in large urns filled the air with rich, inviting aromas that mixed with the sweetness of glazed doughnuts and the cream that was always available for those who wanted it. For children on summer break, whose families were managing tight budgets, these refreshments represented more than just snacks; they were reliable sources of nutrition that ensured no young person would be hungry while learning about justice and democracy.

Brown Chapel was located immediately next door to the George Washington Carver housing project where many families with children lived. It naturally became a regular gathering place that drew dozens of children daily. Many came initially for the doughnuts and the opportunity to socialize with friends, but they stayed for the discussions, the contagious singing, and the growing understanding that they were witnessing something larger and more important than their individual concerns.

The beauty of this arrangement was that children could absorb crucial lessons about organizing, strategy, and collective action without feeling like we were being subjected to formal instruction. We learned by listening to adult conversations, by joining in freedom songs that taught both musical and political literacy, and by watching how communities worked together to address shared problems.

The realization that children could be significant participants in these gatherings spread quickly through Selma's young people. They discovered that their presence was not just tolerated but welcomed, that adults understood their energy and idealism were crucial elements of any movement that hoped to create lasting change. Children brought enthusiasm, fearlessness, and a natural sense of justice that hadn't yet been worn down by years of adjustment to inequity.

The meetings themselves had developed their own rites of freedom songs, strategic planning, and cooperative devotion. Each gathering would begin with singing that transformed individual voices into a unified expression of hope and determination. Then came reports on recent developments, discussions of upcoming activities, and always the careful work of ensuring that everyone understood both the goals they were pursuing and the risks they were accepting.

The music at these gatherings was as important as the speeches and planning sessions. Freedom songs filled Brown Chapel and the other churches, creating unity through shared voice and rhythm. The children quickly memorized the basic anthems that everyone knew by heart—a set of songs that turned old spirituals into assertions of perseverance and courageous defiance.

Reverend Hosea Williams was particularly known for leading "All Things Are Possible, If You Only Believe," his powerful voice drawing everyone into the call-and-response mode that made singing a combined effort rather than individual performance. The children's voices blended with adults in songs that had been adapted from spirituals, labor movement anthems, and newly composed freedom declarations. Each one taught movement philosophy through memorable melodies that could be learned quickly and remembered forever, much like the Latin liturgy at Saint Elizabeth Church and the educational songs in the school.

These weren't just songs for enjoyment. They served multiple essential purposes in the movement's success. Songs like "Ain't Gonna Let Nobody Turn Me 'Round" built courage before dangerous marches, helping participants face police violence and hostile crowds. "Keep Your Eyes on the Prize" maintained morale during long planning sessions that stretched late into the night. "This Little Light of Mine" created spiritual grounding that connected each individual to the movement's work and to deep faith traditions, reminding everyone that they were engaged in sacred work. The lyrics themselves became teaching tools, conveying movement goals and philosophy in ways that could be remembered and repeated long after meetings ended.

The call-and-response structure was particularly powerful for bringing everyone into participation. Even the youngest children could join in immediately, their voices adding to the collective power and hope. This wasn't passive listening but active formation of the solidarity that sustained the movement through setbacks and dangers.

The other children and I absorbed these songs through repetition, learning not only the words but also how music could turn a roomful of individuals into a single force for change. Years after leaving Selma, the sound of any of these tunes would immediately take us back to Brown Chapel, to what it felt like to be part of something bigger than ourselves, reminding us that social change demanded not only strategy and sacrifice but also whatever joy and hope singing together could muster.

Freedom Songs of the Selma Movement
The songs most frequently heard at mass meetings included:

Core Movement Anthems:

- *We Shall Overcome*
- *Ain't Gonna Let Nobody Turn Me 'Round*
- *Which Side Are You On?*
- *All Things Are Possible (If You Only Believe)*

Spiritual-Based Freedom Songs:

- *This Little Light of Mine*
- *Woke Up This Morning with My Mind Set on Freedom*
- *I'm on My Way to Freedom Land*
- *Oh Freedom*
- *Keep Your Eyes on the Prize*
- *Before I'll Be a Slave*
- *Walk Together Children*

Call-and-Response Songs:

- *Everybody Sing Freedom*
- *Freedom Is a Constant Struggle*
- *I Love Everybody in My Heart*
- *We Are Not Afraid*
- *Hallelujah, I'm A-Traveling*

Movement Adaptations:

- *We Shall Not Be Moved*
- *Go Tell It on the Mountain (Freedom's Coming)*
- *Marching 'Round Selma*
- *Ain't Scared of Your Jail*

"We don't expect anybody to do anything they're not comfortable with," the organizers would stress. "But we are asking everyone to seriously consider what kind of community it is they want to live in, and how much they are willing to endure or put up with."

For me, these meetings were the practical application of everything I had been learning through my altar boy service and my education at Saint Elizabeth. The Catholic social teaching that emphasized justice for the oppressed was being translated into specific actions designed to challenge specific injustices. The Latin responses that spoke of serving God were finding their expression in service to the community's most vulnerable members.

But the transition from attending meetings to participating in direct action required a different kind of courage and commitment. It was one thing to sing freedom songs in the safety of familiar churches—it was another thing entirely to walk through Selma's streets carrying signs or attempting to register to vote at a courthouse protected by hostile law enforcement. The neighborhood that had fostered Carrie's children—the nurturing community of relatives, neighbors, store owners, teachers, and ministers—had protected us from the worst harms of segregated society. Yet participating in the movement required us to step out of that protective space and into the fray of the civil rights movement.

Looking back years later, I would come to believe that without the dedicated involvement of young people and adolescents, the movement in Selma might not have ever been successful. Children and teenagers brought something to the struggle that adults, with their greater understanding of potential consequences, sometimes found difficult to maintain: a willingness to take risks based on simple moral clarity rather than complex political calculations.

In many ways, young people like Joan, Yolanda, Tena, Elaine and I served as stand-ins for parents who couldn't afford to participate directly in civil rights activities. Adults with jobs that could be lost, mortgages that could be foreclosed, or businesses that could be looted or shut down, faced economic retaliation that could destroy their families' security. But children could attend meetings, participate in marches, and engage in civil disobedience with consequences that, while serious, were less likely to result in family devastation. We could afford to be arrested, to miss school for demonstrations, and to challenge authority in ways that our parents, with greater responsibilities and vulnerabilities, often could not. This dynamic created a situation where the most visible and committed participants in Selma's civil rights activities were young people who brought both moral authority and practical freedom to the movement.

The children also brought a different kind of credibility to the movement's activities. When television cameras and newspaper photographers captured images of young people, some as young as ten, being attacked by police officers or harassed by hostile crowds, the moral contrast was stark and undeniable. Children singing freedom songs while being teargassed or clubbed created the kind of visual narrative that forced observers to choose sides in ways that might not have been as clear if only adults had been involved.

Yet the children were not just pawns in a strategic game. We were getting an education in democracy, organization, and collective action that no classroom could have given us. We learned that to be successful we had to bring together different groups, sustain a commitment for long periods of time, and resolve differences and conflicts within our group. But the lesson that I think was the hardest was how to keep hope alive given many setbacks and disappointments.

We also learned that social change required both courage and discipline, both idealism and practical planning. The freedom songs that seemed so joyful and spontaneous were carefully chosen to build unity and maintain morale. The mass meetings, which may have seemed unordered to young participants, were highly organized efforts to coordinate complex activities involving hundreds of people across multiple organizations.

Most importantly, we learned that democracy did not just happen to us, rather, it is something we made through our own action and commitment. We found out that citizenship was something more than voting as soon as you hit the awaited age of eighteen; it was taking ownership for the welfare of your community from the earliest age you can start having an impact.

The children's daily encounters with institutionalized discrimination provided the context that made the mass meetings feel urgent rather than incidental. When Reverend Hosea Williams sang "All Things Are

Possible, If You Only Believe," the children understood exactly what changes needed to become possible: reformations of the divided schools, churches, bathrooms, bus station ticket windows, movie theaters. When speakers talked about dignity and equality, the children could envision specific signs removed, barriers eliminated, and freedoms restored.

The civil rights movement in Selma wasn't fighting against abstract concepts, but against the concrete realities that shaped every trip downtown, every attempt to access public services, every reminder that citizenship came in distinct categories depending on the accident of birth that determined skin color.

The first major test of this courage came on a day that none of the participants fully understood would become known to history as Bloody Sunday. The children gathered at Brown Chapel on March 7, 1965, with the same anticipation they brought to all movement activities, but without any clear understanding of what they would experience later that day. Our mother, Carrie, was not with us, nor were many of the adults from the neighborhood, but our upbringing had prepared us for this moment.

"We're going to walk to Montgomery," was the simple explanation they received. "We're going to demonstrate that we have the right to move freely in our own state and to petition our government for fair treatment."

The walk started out in the typical way of movement activities—singing, resolve, and that feeling that you have when you are with others who care about something more than themselves. Reverend Hosea Williams, Reverend James Bevel, and other influential community leaders kept the group organized and focused. Joan, Yolanda, and I as well as our cousins entered the procession, flanked by friends, neighbors, and members of the community whose presence made it all seem less intimidating.

What we didn't realize as we started to walk in the direction of the Edmund Pettus Bridge was that our Uncle DeeDee had placed himself near the front of the march, standing right next to John Lewis. Uncle DeeDee also did not realize that we kids were not far behind him. We had no idea that our uncle was showing the same sort of quiet courage that had stayed with our family over a century and generations of obstacles.

The air of excitement and anticipation shifted as we approached the bottom of the backside of the bridge. Officers appeared and shouted commands to turn around, creating confusion and uncertainty among marchers, especially young marchers, who had expected to be able to complete our peaceful demonstration. When the front-line leaders knelt and the rows behind them began to kneel, prayers started with the hope that spiritual authority might provide protection from whatever was about to happen.

Instead, the onslaught began. People were tear-gassed, clubbed, and jabbed with electric cow prods. Police on horseback trampled demonstrators who were trapped with nowhere to go and no way to defend themselves. Men, women, and children, young and old, were chased as they ran back toward Brown Chapel AME Church. Hundreds were injured, and all were traumatized by the violence they had witnessed and experienced.

For me—a twelve-year-old boy—and my sisters and cousins, Bloody Sunday was an introduction to the reality that challenging injustice could provoke responses of shocking brutality. The peaceful march they had joined, with songs and hope, had quickly exploded into a scene of violence that would be broadcast into homes across America and around the world.

"I don't understand why they wanted to hurt us!" Joan exclaimed, as the family gathered that evening to process what had happened. "We weren't trying to hurt anyone. We just wanted to walk to Montgomery."

"Some people are so afraid of change they're willing to use violence to stop it," Carrie answered, her voice carrying the calm authority that helped her children make sense of events that seemed senseless. "But that doesn't mean we stop working for what's right. It means we must be smarter and more determined."

Bloody Sunday initially catapulted Selma and the larger civil rights movement to worldwide attention. Television broadcasts of peaceful protesters being beaten by law enforcement officials provoked a moral crisis that demanded Americans confront the reality of segregation's brutality. For the children who had directly witnessed that violence, it was both traumatic and transformative.

It was only later, after *Time Magazine* ran a March 19, 1965, cover story, that the family read and realized Uncle DeeDee—the fun-loving jokester from a few houses down, frequenter of backyard barbecues and pea shelling parties—was the one featured prominently in the photograph that would become one of the most recognizable images of the civil rights movement. There he was, positioned next to John Lewis, sporting his fishing hat, trench coat, and ever-present cigar stub, always easily identifiable to relatives who had seen him at countless family gatherings.

The planning for the second march to Montgomery began immediately, but this time the preparation was more intensive, and the stakes were clearly understood by everyone involved. The violence of Bloody Sunday had demonstrated that peaceful protest could provoke brutal responses, but it had also proven that such responses would not stop the movement from advancing.

"We're going back," the organizers announced at the next mass meeting. "We're going to complete the march we started, and we're going to do it with even more people than before. The entire world is watching now, and we're going to show them what courage looks like."

For me, however, deciding to join the second march called for a different sort of deliberation than that raised by the first. Now I knew the potential. Now I knew that walking across the Edmund Pettus Bridge could mean facing violence, arrest, or injury. The decision to be involved had to be made with all the possible consequences in mind.

"I'm scared," I told my mother as we talked through my decision to take part. "But I'm more afraid of what will happen if we don't keep fighting."

"That's courage," Carrie responded. "Not the absence of fear, but the will to do what is right in the face of it."

The second march proceeded very differently from the first. Martin Luther King Jr., Ralph Abernathy, Andrew Young, C. T. Vivian, and other notable civil rights leaders joined Reverend Williams and Reverend Bevel in heading the march. This time there were clergy from various denominations joining the procession, demonstrating that the struggle for civil rights had moral support that transcended racial and religious boundaries. As I walked toward the back of the procession, I was astonished by what I saw.

Up until then, I was only familiar with Baptist, Lutheran, Catholic, Methodist, Seventh-day Adventist, and Jehovah's Witnesses. Now I was seeing denominations that I had never seen or heard of, and other kinds of priests and nuns clothed differently from anything that I had ever seen or imagined.

This diversity of faith traditions united in common cause provided a powerful lesson about the universal nature of justice. The civil rights movement wasn't just a political struggle. It was a moral crusade that attracted support from people whose only common ground was their commitment to human dignity and equal treatment.

But even as this great gathering of various faiths and people helped bring about the needed change of heart in the country, the marchers faced reminders of how deep the divisions ran. Often during the march, I was confused by the young white kids who violently mocked and cursed us from across the street or on the sidewalks. They all seemed so angry—where and how could these young kids get so much anger? The marchers had done nothing to them, and they didn't even know them.

The contrast was jarring: clergy from many denominations walking together in peaceful solidarity all around me and my siblings and cousins, while children our own age screamed hatred from the sidelines. It was one thing to understand that adults disagreed about civil rights, but the venom from children who should have been playing rather than hating was harder to comprehend.

Later, as a young adult in the working world, even in corporate conference rooms, a thought would always come to my mind: *Those young people who were mocking and yelling at us, where are they today?* Sometimes I imagined I could hear those voices deep within the country's politics and political divisions, the same anger and hatred, the same resistance to change, the same unwillingness to see others as fully human.

It was this great gathering of various faiths and people that would help to bring about the needed change of heart in our country. I have come to believe that, even today, for any profound changes in our country to take place, the same coming together of people of different faiths and backgrounds will have to happen.

The second march to Montgomery was also functionally significant beyond its symbolic value. It was evidence that organized, disciplined, nonviolent action could triumph over violent resistance if it had a moral authority and wide popular base. For the children who took part in both marches, it was evidence that our bravery and conviction could help bring about significant social change.

But the most unforgettable moment of the whole Montgomery march experience came to be known as "The Night the Stars Came Out in Alabama." I had no idea what awaited the gatherers near Montgomery as they made their way to the Saint Jude Catholic Campus.

What I discovered was a gathering of entertainment figures unlike anything I had ever imagined possible. Nina Simone, Harry Belafonte, Aretha Franklin, James Brown, Sammy Davis Jr., Peter, Paul and Mary, Joan Baez, all the singers and entertainers I listened to on Selma's two radio stations, WJAM and WTQX, were performing in the rain-soaked fields of Alabama in support of the civil rights movement.

I couldn't believe it was happening. All the many singers and entertainers that I listened to on the radio were out here tonight. I suppose I was, at twelve years old, what one might call a Top 40 aficionado, and now they were all here supporting the same cause we had been working for.

This convergence of popular culture and social activism demonstrated something important about the civil rights movement—it had captured the moral imagination of the country in ways that transcended politics or regional interests. The same voices that provided soundtracks for teenage life were now providing the soundtrack for social transformation.

The march from Selma to Montgomery had accomplished something unprecedented: It had forced a national conversation about voting rights and racial justice that would result in federal legislation protecting the rights that demonstrators had been demanding. For the children who had participated in these historic events, it was proof that young people could play meaningful roles in shaping their country's future.

But the most profound impact was on our understanding of what citizenship demanded. We had learned that democracy was not a spectator sport, that justice insisted upon active participation, and that individuals could contribute to collective change when they were willing to accept the risks and responsibilities that meaningful action necessitated.

The foundation laid through altar boy service, Saint Elizabeth education, and an upbringing under our mother Carrie had prepared us for this moment—the discipline, the courage, the commitment to service, and the understanding that faith required action. Now we had applied those lessons in service of something larger than ourselves, and we had seen that such service could produce results that changed the world.

Soon the family would move from Selma to Atlanta, taking with us not only our scholastic and spiritual formation but also the lesson that when justice needed you, you could play a part in changing history. No longer just "Carrie's kids," but young people who'd helped to write American history.

CHAPTER TEN

Raised to Fly

I know that there are some of my children who feel I loved one more than another—that is not true. There is a special place in my heart for each of you.

—Carrie Louise, Sept. 28, 1998

By 1966, with nine children ranging from six-year-old twins Christopher and Anthony to nineteen-year-old Gwendolyn, the house at 1421 Sylvan Street had become a laboratory for one of the most remarkable experiments in parenting that Selma had ever witnessed. Carrie's approach to raising children during the volatile civil rights era defied conventional wisdom about protection, authority, and the proper relationship between parents and children in dangerous times.

"I'm not raising children to stay children," she would tell neighbors who worried about the freedom she gave her sons and daughters to make their own decisions about participating in movement activities. "I'm raising children to become adults who can think for themselves and do what's right even when it's difficult or dangerous."

This philosophy had been tested repeatedly as her children grew older and the civil rights movement intensified around them. While many parents kept their children close to home during demonstrations and mass meetings, Carrie allowed hers to participate fully in activities that could result in arrest, injury, or economic retaliation against the family, as she demonstrated on Bloody Sunday.

Yet her approach wasn't permissive or careless; it was highly deliberate, because she understood that children protected from moral dilemmas would be ill prepared for the moral ambiguities they would encounter both as young adults and over their adult lives. She was raising children to lead in a rapidly changing world, and leaders had always needed both courage and judgment, both of which only came from experience.

"The world my children are growing up in is different from the world I grew up in," she explained to Dr. Dumont during one of their conversations about the family's civil rights activities. "They're going to have opportunities I never had, but they're also going to face challenges I never faced. I must prepare them for both."

This preparation took many forms, but the most important was the way she handled her children's questions and concerns about the movement activities they were witnessing and participating in. Rather than providing simple answers or dismissing their worries, she engaged them in serious conversations about justice, courage, and the responsibilities that came with being part of a community working for change.

No single example better demonstrated Carrie's faith in her children's judgment and integrity than the responsibility she gave to Gwendolyn every Saturday afternoon. Rather than handling the family's financial obligations herself, Carrie would endorse the back of her paycheck and hand it to her eldest daughter along with a carefully prepared list of everything that needed to be accomplished downtown. Carrie gave this responsibility to Gwendolyn starting when she was just fourteen.

"Pay bills first," was always Carrie's instruction as she sent Gwendolyn off to manage the family's weekly finances. The list was methodical and precise: payments to Eagle's Department Store, Sears Roebuck, Alabama

Power and Light Company, Alabama Gas Company, and finally, with whatever money remained, grocery shopping at Delchamps using the detailed shopping list Carrie had prepared.

This wasn't a small responsibility or a symbolic gesture; it was trusting a teenager with the family's survival. If Gwendolyn made poor decisions, bought unnecessary items, or failed to prioritize correctly, nine children and their mother would go without electricity, heat, or food. The trust was absolute, and the consequences were immediate and real.

The arrangement taught lessons that no classroom could provide. Gwendolyn learned about budgeting under pressure, the difference between wants and needs, and the weight of responsibility that came with other people depending on your judgment. She discovered what it felt like to make decisions that affected not just herself but everyone she loved.

"It used to hurt my heart," Gwendolyn would remember years later. "I'd get back home and I'd say, 'Mommie, you only have thirty-five cents left from your paycheck,' and she'd say to me, 'Did you do everything that I asked you to do with the money?' I would say, 'Yes, Mommie, I did.' She would say, 'Then it's all right. That's what it was for. You did good.'"

These Saturday afternoon conversations revealed both the reality of their economic circumstances and the grace with which Carrie handled financial pressure. She never expressed frustration about having only thirty-five cents left from a week's wages, never suggested that Gwendolyn should have somehow stretched the money further, never complained about the impossibility of supporting ten people on a nurse's salary.

Instead, she focused on whether the work had been done correctly and completely. If the bills were paid and groceries purchased according to the list, then the mission was successful regardless of how little money remained. This response taught Gwendolyn that responsible people fulfilled their obligations first and worried about personal satisfaction second.

The trust also created natural accountability that was more powerful than any punishment could have been. Gwendolyn understood that careless spending or poor judgment would immediately affect her younger siblings' wellbeing. The direct connection between individual responsibility and collective welfare created motivation for careful decision-making that came from love rather than fear.

But more than that, the lesson affirmed Carrie's belief in her daughter's character and ability. Teenagers her age were begging their parents for money to go out, while Gwendolyn was balancing a family budget and handling financial responsibilities that most adults found daunting. It was a burden and an honor, and it proved that Carrie saw her eldest daughter not as a child who needed excessive protection but rather as a young adult who could handle sizable responsibilities.

The Saturday routine continued for years, creating weekly opportunities for Gwendolyn to practice the kind of judgment and responsibility she would need throughout her adult life. When she eventually left for college and later law school, she carried with her confidence that came from knowing she could manage whatever challenges arose, because she had already proven herself capable of managing many important responsibilities.

Years later, when Gwendolyn became a successful lawyer and judge, she would credit these Saturday afternoon expeditions with teaching her more about responsibility, integrity, and practical decision-making than any formal education she had received. The trust Carrie had placed in her as a teenager had created capabilities and confidence that served her throughout her professional career.

The kitchen lessons and sewing demonstrations were just part of a larger education in self-reliance and competence that Carrie was providing through daily expectations and steady guidance. She believed that children needed to learn practical skills that would serve them throughout their lives, and she made no distinction between "men's work" and "women's work." There was only what needed doing and who was old enough to do it properly.

Year-round daily chores were assigned by capability rather than gender. The boys were responsible for taking out trash and keeping the yard raked and cleared of debris, but they also learned to sort laundry, wash dishes, and iron their own clothes. The girls managed cooking responsibilities and younger children's care, but they also learned outdoor maintenance and basic repairs.

Everyone had to master the complete cycle of laundry: sorting by color and fabric type, washing at appropriate temperatures, hanging clothes to dry on outside lines, bringing them in when properly dried, ironing what needed pressing, and folding everything before putting it away. Everyone learned to wash dishes, keep their rooms tidy, and look after anyone younger than themselves.

In summers, when school was out and time was available for deeper cleaning, all the children had duties scrubbing floors and washing walls and windows. After Saturday morning cartoons ended, going out to play was allowed only after the house was entirely cleaned and in order. By the time cleaning was finished, everything would smell of Pine-Sol and vinegar, the institutional aromas of cleanliness that Carrie insisted upon.

"I'm so proud of how hard you work," she would tell them when inspection revealed properly completed chores. "You're learning to take responsibility for your environment, and that's going to serve you well your entire lives."

The praise wasn't empty encouragement; it was recognition of real accomplishment and developing competence. The children learned to feel pleased and proud of their own work, understanding that quality effort produced visible results and earned genuine appreciation.

Carrie's household expectations were not negotiable. She believed that cleanliness was a kind of dignity and discipline, a form of love expressed through creating order and beauty in their immediate environment. Every room in the house bore her mark: fresh linens, swept corners, and folded towels. The children rotated through dishwashing duty, took turns stirring beans on the stove, and helped roll out dough for biscuits when extra mouths were coming to dinner.

For particularly disliked chores, informal trading systems developed. I would often trade places with Yolanda when it was her turn to wash dishes, a task she genuinely hated, in exchange for her taking one of my responsibilities that I found equally tedious. These negotiations taught the children about cooperation, compromise, and the reality that different people found different tasks more or less tolerable.

But beyond the practical skills and work discipline, these daily expectations created intimate moments that revealed different dimensions of family relationships and individual personalities. Sometimes late in the evening, after a particularly long day at the clinic, Carrie would ask me to massage her aching legs.

The varicose veins from standing long hours every day at work caused her real pain, and she would come home visibly tired and hurting. I felt sorry for her, seeing how hard she worked and how much discomfort she endured to provide for us. But I also felt honored that she would ask me, her oldest son, to perform this small service that would help her feel better.

As I worked to ease the pain in her tired legs, she would sometimes talk about her day—preparing prescription packages, drawing blood, administering vaccinations and other shots, consulting with patients to explain the doctor's instructions. These conversations gave me glimpses into her professional life and helped me understand the important work she was doing beyond just being our mother.

When PTA meeting nights came around at Saint Elizabeth, I would walk to school with Mommie to talk with the nuns and pick up report cards. I never minded these walks because I had good relationships with my teachers and generally expected straight A's. But what I valued most were the walks home, when she would tell me that we were all doing well in school and that she was very proud of us.

These individual moments—walking together in the evening, having her undivided attention, hearing her pride expressed directly to me rather than to all the children collectively—created bonds that were different from the group experience of being one of nine children. They showed me that despite the demands of managing such a large family, she saw me as an individual with my own achievements and character.

The lessons in self-reliance that Carrie taught through daily expectations would prove their value in unexpected ways years later. When I was doing laundry at the college laundromat, women present would stare and marvel at the knowledge and efficiency with which I sorted, washed, dried, and folded my clothes. What seemed remarkable to them was just common knowledge you got from growing up with Carrie, the natural result of years of doing it properly under her instruction and supervision.

The same proved true for cooking, cleaning, and general household management. Carrie's children left 1421 Sylvan Street equipped with practical skills that many of their peers had never developed, particularly young men who had been raised with the expectation that domestic work was women's responsibility. Carrie's insistence that competence knew no gender boundaries had created young adults who could manage their own lives independently regardless of their living situations.

But perhaps the most important lesson embedded in all these daily expectations and practical skills was about dignity and self-respect. Carrie was teaching her children that taking care of yourself and your environment wasn't drudgery or mere necessity; it was a form of self-love and respect for the space you inhabited. Clean clothes, nourishing food, orderly rooms—these weren't luxuries but expressions of the belief that you deserved to live with dignity regardless of your economic circumstances.

When ten-year-old Sherman asked permission to board a church bus and travel to Atlanta for Dr. Martin Luther King Jr.'s funeral in 1968, many parents would have said no without hesitation. A ten-year-old traveling to another state without family supervision, during a time of national mourning and potential unrest, would have seemed an unnecessary risk.

But Carrie knew that Sherman's plea was more than a child wanting an adventure. He wanted to honor a leader whose teachings formed the core of his understanding of justice and nonviolence. He wanted to be part of a historic moment that would put the loss of someone who had inspired his family's dedication to social change in perspective.

"Do you understand what you're asking to do?" she asked him as they discussed his request. "Do you understand that this trip is about more than just going somewhere new?"

"Yes, Mommie. Dr. King was important to all of us, and I want to be there when people say goodbye to him."

"And do you understand that you'll be representing our family and everything we believe in while you're away?"

"Yes, Mommie. I'll behave the way you taught me to behave."

That was enough. Carrie gave her permission, understanding that this experience would contribute more to Sherman's moral development than any lecture she could give about history, leadership, or social responsibility. She was raising children to engage with the world rather than hide from it, and such engagement sometimes required taking calculated risks.

This same philosophy governed her response to her children's participation in civil rights demonstrations, even after the violence of Bloody Sunday had demonstrated the physical dangers such participation could involve. While some parents pulled their children back from movement activities after witnessing the brutality that peaceful protesters could face, Carrie continued to allow her children to make their own decisions about participation.

"Are you sure you want to do this?" she would ask before major demonstrations. "Are you prepared for whatever might happen?"

When they said yes, she respected their judgment and supported their choice, understanding that courage was something that had to be chosen freely rather than imposed from outside. She was teaching them that moral action required personal commitment, not just obedience to authority.

But the most challenging test of this parenting philosophy came in 1967, during my first year at R. B. Hudson High School, when I found myself thrown into a situation that required me to choose between peer pressure and the values my mother had instilled in me.

It was early in the morning, and I was in my first period Physical Science class with Mr. Jones when the sound of roaring voices approached from down the hallway. The noise grew louder and more urgent until the entire class sprang up and joined the clamoring students rushing toward the exit.

Before I fully understood what was happening, I found myself outside the school building, swept along by a crowd of students rushing toward the small Minit Shop convenience store adjacent to the campus. To my shock and dismay, I watched my classmates storm the little store and begin chaotically raking all the products off the shelves in an act of unorganized destruction.

The shop owner, who was white or Jewish, had never harmed or been unkind to the students as far as I knew. The Minit Shop was simply a place where kids purchased candy and snacks before and after school, a normal part of our daily routine that had nothing to do with the civil rights struggles that were transforming their community.

Standing in chaos, watching my classmates destroy property and intimidate an innocent shopkeeper, I faced a moment of moral choice that would test everything my mother had taught me about right and wrong, justice and violence, individual conscience, and peer pressure.

Long before I heard Dr. King or anyone speak of nonviolence, I already knew my position on this matter. It went without saying. It was a natural part of my upbringing under Carrie, and in the Catholic faith.

While my classmates continued their destructive rampage, I stood apart, refusing to participate despite the peer pressure to join in. I watched in astonishment but made no move to take anything or contribute to the destruction. My conscience, shaped by years of Carrie's teaching and Catholic formation, would not allow me to participate in violence against innocent people, even when everyone around me was doing so.

The incident was brief but memorable, a spontaneous explosion of anger and frustration that dissipated as quickly as it began. But for me, it represented a defining moment in my moral development, a test of whether the values my mother had instilled would hold firm under the pressure of peer expectations and collective action.

Walking home that afternoon, I reflected on what had happened and why I had chosen differently from my classmates. The answer lay in everything Carrie had taught me about the difference between justice and revenge, between righteous anger and destructive violence, between standing up for what was right and simply acting out in frustration.

"Mommie," I said that evening as we talked about my day, "something happened at school today that I need to tell you about."

As I described the Minit Shop incident and my decision not to participate, Carrie listened with the attention she always gave to her children's moral struggles. When I finished, she nodded with the satisfaction of a parent whose teaching had been validated under pressure.

"You did the right thing," she said simply. "It's easy to do what's right when everyone else is doing what's right. The real test is whether you'll do what's right when everyone else is doing what's wrong."

This conversation reinforced the lesson that Carrie had been teaching all her children through her approach to the civil rights movement—that moral action required individual conscience, not just group participation. That justice was about creating positive change, not just expressing anger. That nonviolence was a principle that applied even when violence seemed easier or more satisfying.

The Minit Shop incident also demonstrated how Carrie's parenting philosophy created children who could think independently even under intense peer pressure. By giving us practice making moral decisions in less challenging situations, she had prepared us to make good decisions when the stakes were higher and the pressure more intense.

"I'm proud of you for standing up for what you believed was right," she told me. "That's what I've been trying to teach all of you—that you have to be able to live with your own conscience, regardless of what other people think you should do."

This ability to act according to conscience rather than peer pressure would serve all of Carrie's children well as we moved into adulthood and faced moral challenges in our professional and personal lives. The freedom she had given us to make our own decisions during childhood and adolescence had developed our capacity for moral reasoning and independent judgment.

The results of this parenting philosophy were evident in how we handled the countless challenges we faced growing up in Selma during the 1960s. We developed confidence in our abilities, respect for others' dignity, commitment to justice, and the kind of moral courage that would serve us throughout our lives.

When Yolanda decided at the age of twenty that she wanted to travel to California with no clear plan beyond getting away from familiar circumstances, other parents might have refused or tried to change her mind about such a reckless decision. But Carrie understood that her daughter needed to test her independence and discover her own capabilities.

"Who do you know, and where will you stay?" she asked when Yolanda announced her intention to buy a one-way ticket to anywhere west for $100 or less.

"I don't know anyone. I really thought I could stay on the beach," was Yolanda's honest answer.

Rather than forbidding the trip or lecturing about its dangers, Carrie quietly arranged for Yolanda to stay with her friend Mae Watts in Riverside, California, providing safety without undermining her daughter's sense of independence and adventure.

"What I know now and remember most," Yolanda would reflect years later, "is that Mommie knew all her children well. She encouraged us and believed that we were well grounded. She helped me to be brave and an independent thinker."

This was the essence of Carrie's parenting philosophy—knowing each of us well enough to understand what we needed for healthy development, providing guidance without controlling our choices, and trusting that the foundation she had laid would enable us to make good decisions even in challenging circumstances.

The approach required enormous faith in her children's capabilities and judgment, but it also demonstrated enormous respect for our individual dignity and potential. Rather than seeing us as property to be protected or problems to be managed, she saw us as people in the process of becoming who we were meant to be.

"I'm not trying to keep my children safe from the world," she would explain to people who questioned her permissive approach to their civil rights activities and other potentially risky choices. "I'm trying to prepare them to make the world safer for everyone."

This preparation involved exposing them to moral challenges that would develop their character, giving them practice making important decisions, and ensuring they understood the difference between freedom and license, between independence and irresponsibility.

The results spoke for themselves. By the time the family prepared to leave Selma for Atlanta in 1968, Carrie had raised children who were academically prepared for any educational opportunity, morally prepared for any ethical challenge, and personally prepared for leadership roles in whatever fields we chose to pursue.

We were young people who understood that privilege came with responsibility, that individual success required contributing to collective advancement, and that the greatest achievement was using our gifts in service of others who needed help. We had been raised not just to succeed, but to fly—to soar beyond the limitations our society had tried to impose and to lift others as we climbed.

The philosophy that had seemed radical to some of our neighbors had proven itself through results that would last generations. Carrie had indeed raised her children to fly, and we would spend the rest of our lives proving that her faith in our potential had been justified.

CHAPTER ELEVEN

Courtship of Courage

The introduction came through Mrs. Ida Bennett, Carrie's colleague at Dr. Dumont's clinic. Mrs. Ida had been watching her friend navigate single motherhood with nine children and wondering if there might be a way to bring some companionship into her carefully ordered life. It was 1967, and Carrie had been managing alone for a decade since Clarence Sr. left for Cleveland. She had built a reputation as someone who could manage any challenge, but Mrs. Ida saw she also deserved support in return.

"I want you to meet someone," Mrs. Ida said one afternoon as they finished seeing the last patients of the day. "There's going to be a class reunion dance, and I have a friend who's coming home to Selma for the first time in twenty years. I think you two might enjoy each other's company."

Mrs. Ida's friend was Horace Hunter, a man who had left Selma years ago and joined the U.S. Merchant Marines, where he had spent decades traveling the world's oceans and building projects in distant cities while gaining experiences and perspectives that few people in

Selma could imagine. When not at sea, he had also made his living as a general contractor and builder in Seattle, Washington.

"I'm not sure, Ida," Carrie replied, thinking of the complications that any romantic relationship would bring to her already complex life. "I've got nine children and responsibilities that don't leave much time for social activities and starting any kind of romantic relationships."

Immediately responding to Carrie's uncertainty, Mrs. Ida declared, "But that's all the more reason you should consider the dance and a chance to meet some adult company. You've been looking after everyone but yourself for years. And maybe it's finally someone else's turn to take care of you?"

The reunion dance was at one of Selma's social nightclubs, and Carrie found herself in the unusual position of attending a social event without any of her children or any medical responsibilities requiring her attention. She had dressed in her best evening gown, conscious that this evening was unlike any other she had experienced in quite some time.

For Carrie's children, the entire matter of another man in their mother's life was about as unexpected and concerning as the arrival of their third brother Sherman had been years earlier. They were not particularly interested in this new possibility, and the younger children especially were not always privy to the adult conversations that surrounded such decisions.

At least two other men had tried to court Carrie before Horace Hunter's arrival on the scene. Although these suitors certainly saw her as an intelligent, tall, attractive woman, they also had to deal with the reality that she came with nine children—a responsibility that would have intimidated most men.

It would be something of a miracle, by anyone's measure, if there were any man who dared to marry any woman with nine children, regardless of how attractive he found Carrie herself. But Carrie was no ordinary woman. She was a pillar of the community, liked and well-regarded by her neighbors for the medical care she gave and how she had raised her children. She'd shown her ability, her integrity, and her love for family in ways that were plain to anyone who knew or met her.

Gwendolyn and Carolyn, being older, could understand implicitly what their mother's possible remarriage meant in a practical sense. They saw the financial strain of raising nine children on a nurse's salary, the physical exhaustion in working and then running a household all day and night, and the loneliness of having so much primary responsibility for so many lives without anyone to share that burden.

But the younger kids, especially the second set of twins and Sherman, had a hard time understanding why their family, which seemed to be running just fine as it was, needed to change. They had created systems and relationships that were comfortable and predictable, living in the comfort of Mommie being the sun in their universe. The prospect of adding a stepfather into their world seemed, well, threatening more than promising.

Horace Hunter was not really what Carrie had expected. Distinguished-looking and well-built, though slightly shorter than Carrie herself, he carried himself with the confidence that came from years of navigating both literal and figurative storms. But there was also a gentleness about him, a respectful attention that suggested he understood the significance of meeting a woman who had accomplished what Carrie had.

"Mrs. Ida says you're a nurse and midwife," he said when they were introduced. "Well, that sounds hard especially since you've got your own family to look after."

"It's time-consuming," Carrie said, studying this man who had lived such a different life than anyone she knew. "Mrs. Ida tells me that you cruise the world with the Merchant Marine."

"I do. I've seen ports in Central America, the South Pacific, everywhere. But I've never lived anywhere that has felt like home the way Selma does."

Their subsequent conversation was free-flowing and unforced, like time between old friends. Carrie thought to herself, *He's a man who hadn't used his travels as an excuse from all that he'd left behind in Selma, but rather as a way into the world beyond it.* He spoke of the various cultures he'd seen and eaten with, the construction projects he'd overseen, even the loneliness that accompanied a life on the move without an established community.

But he also demonstrated genuine interest in Carrie's life and work, asking thoughtful questions about her medical practice, her children's education, and her experiences raising a large family during the civil rights movement and all that was going on in Selma. He seemed to understand that any relationship with her would mean accepting not just her individual affections but her commitments to her children and community.

"I've got to ask," she said later in the evening, "are you prepared for someone who comes with nine children and professional responsibilities that don't follow a normal schedule?"

"I've spent two decades adjusting to whatever circumstances demanded," he said. "I think I could learn to adapt to a life that included your family and the work you do."

The dance concluded with mutual interest but also the practical understanding that any further getting to know each other had to happen through letters and phone calls. Horace's Merchant Marine schedule would send him back out to sea within days, and Carrie's responsibilities made travel impossible. If anything was going to come of them, it'd have to survive through long distance.

Within weeks, Carrie's daily excursions to the mailbox at 1421 Sylvan Street had a fresh meaning. Air mail special delivery letters with their identifying red, white, and blue striped borders began to arrive in regular jets postmarked from ports all over Central America and the South Pacific. It was the first time in years that she had looked forward to checking the mail not for medical correspondence or family business, but for personal letters that connected her to someone who was thinking about her from thousands of miles away.

The children soon sensed the importance of this new correspondence, especially when the letters bore colorful stamps from places like Panama, Costa Rica, Nicaragua, El Salvador, New Zealand, and Australia. To us, the stamps were treasures for our collections, but the letters themselves hinted at something more mysterious—that perhaps changes, unknown to us, were happening.

I probingly asked my mother—with what she knew to be only natural curiosity—as I added another exotic stamp to my collection, "Who's writing to you from all these different places?"

"Just a friend of Mrs. Ida's that I met at a dance a couple of weekends ago. He wants to get to know us better." Carrie withheld what she needed to while understanding her children's natural curiosity about this new change in our lives.

Horace's letters exuded a sense of credibility and demonstrated his character through the written word. He wrote about the places he was visiting, the work he was doing, and his observations of new cultures and their lifestyles. He also wrote about how he had come to appreciate Carrie's life and respect what she had done in Selma.

The letters also revealed a man who was thinking about the logistics of blending two vastly different lives. Horace wrote about his vision for a life that would make room for both his career and her obligations, and for his background and her community service. He wrote about his savings, his business plans, his ideas about where the family might relocate, and his understanding of what it would take to provide educational opportunities for eight children with unique needs and interests. He wasn't asking Carrie to choose between her current life and a life with him; he was proposing ways his resources and skills could improve the life she had already created.

"I've been doing a lot of thinking as to what it would mean if I got married and maybe settled down some place," he wrote in one letter. "I saved enough to buy a house and start a business. And I've picked up enough about building and construction to create my own opportunities anywhere. I've even been looking at school systems in cities where my contracting work could provide steady income. Atlanta has possibilities, and I've started researching Georgia building codes. I guess what I haven't done, up until now, is found a reason to stop traveling and to live my life with someone."

For months, the letters continued back and forth between Horace and Carrie as they courted with due pragmatism. It wasn't just that he was basically telling her how much it would cost him to marry her and how he envisaged things working out financially. Now he was going to be the custodian for nine children, most of them teenagers who had strong beliefs about their lives and futures. He would be joining a family deeply intertwined in the life of Selma, a family dedicated to service that extended well beyond self-interest.

Horace wasn't just writing to Carrie for its own sake, but was also writing about the family he aspired to be a part of, asking intelligent questions about each child's hobbies, progress in school, and personality. He knew that winning Carrie's love would be worthless if he couldn't win her children over.

"Tell me about Clarence Jr.'s altar boy service," he wrote in one letter. "I'd like to understand what that experience means to him and how it's shaping his character."

"How is Sherman adjusting to being the middle child now that the twins are getting older? I remember being the youngest in my family and how that affected my development."

"I know Gwendolyn and Carolyn are attending high school at Holy Rosary Institute. How's that going for them?"

These weren't superficial inquiries designed to impress Carrie with his interest in her children. They represented a serious attempt to understand the family dynamics he would be entering and to begin building individual relationships with each child through their mother's descriptions and responses.

As they continued their long-distance correspondence, their relationship became both deeply personal and practical. Carrie was learning about Horace's character, values, and vision for their potential life together, while he was learning more about the complexities and rewards of joining an established family with strong bonds and elevated aspirations.

But he was also proposing something that might change what the family could do. As a general contractor, he could offer the kind of economic security that had pretty much disappeared since Clarence Sr.'s departure. His travels, which had exposed him to various ways of living, could expand the children's worlds. The fact that he was open to moving meant that new opportunities could be available if the family was willing to reimagine everything.

"I've been thinking about what would be best for the children's future," Carrie told Dr. Dumont during one of their conversations about the developing relationship. "They're all bright and becoming more capable, but they're going to need opportunities that might not be available here in Selma."

"Are you thinking about leaving? Are you sure they would want that?" Dr. Dumont asked, though she had certainly seen this eventuality taking shape as the children aged and their potential became clearer.

"I'm thinking about what would give them the best chance to use their intelligence and their gifts in service of something meaningful," Carrie replied. "If that means leaving Selma, it's worth considering."

Carrie's decision to marry Horace Hunter was the result of the careful thought with which she considered all great decisions in her family. She had a responsibility in Selma, and it wasn't about her happiness or romantic satisfaction; her decision centered on which relationship would most benefit the long-range prospects of her kids and the ongoing projects she had been part of.

When Carrie told Dr. Dumont and Ms. Joan about Horace, her plans to marry him, and the potential move to Georgia, the response was not what she had hoped for from the dear women who had been like surrogate sisters to her for more than two decades. As devout Catholics, Dr. Dumont and Ms. Joan were deeply troubled by Carrie's plans to divorce and remarry. These decisions were obvious contradictions of Catholic teaching that they couldn't support or encourage.

For Carrie, the strain of this conflict was especially painful since it put at risk relationships that carried her across some of the most difficult points in her life. Dr. Dumont and Ms. Joan were not just professional associates, but the women who had enabled her children to go to Saint Elizabeth, who gave her financial assistance when the family needed it most, and who treated her like a member of their family rather than just an employee.

"We cannot continue to support the children's education at Holy

Rosary Institute if you proceed with these plans," Dr. Dumont informed Carrie with the kind of formal tone that signaled how seriously she viewed Carrie's intentions. The message was clear: Choosing to divorce and remarry would mean losing the educational opportunities that had been helping Gwendolyn and Carolyn receive excellent preparation for their futures.

This predicament led Carrie to have to make a tough decision between her own happiness and her children's education. She was well aware of the Catholic position on divorce and remarriage, but she herself was not Catholic, and she also knew that her existence as a single mother of nine required pragmatic solutions that wouldn't always fit in neatly with religious ideals. The isolation, the money stress—and not least the basic human need for companionship and partnership—were real considerations to weigh against the religious obligations of her employers and friends.

The conflict was particularly difficult because Carrie respected Dr. Dumont and Ms. Joan's sincerity and consistency. They weren't imposing arbitrary restrictions but acting according to deeply held beliefs that governed their own lives and choices. Their disappointment wasn't personal vindictiveness but genuine concern about what they saw as moral compromise that could have spiritual consequences.

Carolyn, a junior at Holy Rosary Institute who had developed close bonds with classmates and faculty members, was deeply disappointed at the prospect of having to leave school before graduating. "I was so unhappy," she recalled decades later, "that Mommie told Ms. Joan that if they would let me stay at Holy Rosary and finish school, she would stay with Dr. Dumont until I graduated."

This negotiation revealed both the depth of Carrie's commitment to her children's education and her understanding that relationships built over decades deserved respect and careful handling even during times of disagreement. She was willing to delay her own happiness and postpone major life changes to ensure that Carolyn could complete her education without disruption.

Dr. Dumont and Ms. Joan agreed to this arrangement, allowing Carolyn to complete the latter half of her junior semester followed by her senior year. But because of the demand, Carrie was forced to live with that uncertainty and tension and continue professional relationships that were now somewhat strained by personal choices. For a person who believed in peacefulness and mutual consideration, that season was emotionally exhausting in ways that went well beyond the logistical aspects of wedding preparation and relocation.

The stress on these relationships was a reminder that even the closest bonds could be tested by fundamental conflicts about life choices and moral obligations. It also showed how deeply held religious beliefs, however sincere, could cause clashes between established loyalty and personal circumstances that were hard to reconcile.

But in 1967, as Carrie prepared for marriage while managing the disapproval of women who had been like family to her, the cost of choosing personal happiness over religious conformity felt substantial and lasting. The sacrifice she was making for the chance at a new life included relationships that had sustained her through more than twenty years of professional and personal challenges.

"This is the day," Gwendolyn whispered softly, as the family got ready. "Mommie's going to have a new husband and hopefully we'll move to a new place."

Horace and Carrie were married in 1968 in Carrie's living room at 1421 Sylvan Street. The pastor of Green Street Baptist Church conducted the ceremony, and Carrie's mother Hettie and the neighbor Mrs. Coleman stood as witnesses. It was a quiet affair, without fanfare or pomp. But at the same time, the wedding was intimate, a small gathering of beloved people to commemorate a union built on trust and security.

"Change is never easy, but it's a necessity in order to grow," Carrie was heard saying. "It's certainly brought maturity to each and every one of us as a family. It has broadened our education, and it has given us all the experiences that we've had. While we've been here, we've learned and have given back to the community. We'll see now how we can grow and what else we can do elsewhere."

Since Horace's skills and savings could take the family anywhere, the decision about where to relocate was discussed in the same democratic fashion that Carrie used for other important family decisions. The choice came down to Saint Paul, Minnesota, or Atlanta, Georgia. Saint Paul offered economic opportunities and a climate different from what they had always known. Atlanta offered a growing, diverse economy that could accommodate the different interests and talents that the children were developing, expanding educational options, and a climate more familiar to what they were leaving behind.

"We're going to vote on this as a family," Carrie announced during one of the family meetings where major decisions were made. "Everyone who's old enough to understand the choices gets to express their preference, and we'll make the decision based on what seems best for everyone."

The discussion that followed revealed how much the children had absorbed in thinking about opportunities and challenges. They considered educational options, economic prospects, and the cultural adjustments that would be necessary in either location.

"Atlanta feels more like what we're used to," was one perspective.

"But Minnesota might have opportunities we've never imagined," was another.

In the end, the family chose Atlanta, a decision that would prove transformative for everyone involved.

The preparations for leaving Selma were both practical and emotional. There were arrangements to be made with Dr. Dumont about ending the professional partnership that had sustained Carrie's work for more than twenty years. There were conversations with neighbors about who would continue providing the informal medical care that families had depended on. There were decisions about what to take and what to leave behind.

But most challenging were the conversations with community members who had come to depend on Carrie's presence and availability. For more than two decades, she had been a constant resource for families dealing with medical emergencies, childbirth complications, and the countless health challenges that affected daily life.

"Who's going to deliver babies when you're gone?" Mrs. Coleman asked, expressing the concern that many neighbors felt about losing someone whose skills had kept families alive and healthy.

"There are other midwives in the community," Carrie replied, "and Dr. Dumont will continue providing medical care. You'll still have the resources you need."

But everyone understood that something irreplaceable was being lost. The combination of medical skills, community knowledge, and personal compassion that Carrie brought to her work could not be easily replaced. The family that had anchored Sylvan Street's sense of community and possibility was moving on to opportunities that would take them far from the neighborhood that had shaped their understanding of service and commitment.

In June 1968, ten of the family members piled into the long blue Chrysler station wagon that would carry them to their new life in Atlanta. Gwendolyn was already at Cleveland State University studying Political Science, but the car was packed with everyone else and everything they owned: eight children, two adults, and the accumulated wisdom of more than twenty years of life in Selma, Alabama.

As they drove away from 1421 Sylvan Street, passing the familiar landmarks that had defined their daily routines—Saint Elizabeth Catholic School, Dr. Dumont's clinic, Brown Chapel AME Church—they carried with them more than just personal possessions. They carried the values, experiences, and relationships that had prepared them for whatever challenges and opportunities lay ahead.

The courtship of Horace Hunter had been more than just a romantic relationship. It had been a courtship of courage, a mutual recognition that momentous change required both love and bravery, and both practical preparation and faith in unknown possibilities. The marriage that resulted would provide the foundation for the next chapter of their lives, when the children raised in Selma would discover what they could accomplish when their talents and training were applied to new opportunities in a rapidly changing world.

CHAPTER TWELVE

Atlanta Rising

The long blue Chrysler station wagon rolled through Georgia's summer heat carrying ten members of the Jones family toward a future none of them could fully imagine. The car was packed with clothes, books, Carrie's medical supplies, and the accumulated possessions of a family that had grown from two adults and one baby to a complex household of teenagers, children, and two adults committed to providing them with opportunities that Selma couldn't offer.

Horace drove with the steady confidence of someone who had navigated unfamiliar territories throughout his career, while Carrie sat beside him studying maps and keeping track of the children's needs during the long journey. In the back seats, Carolyn, Yolanda, Joan, Frederick, Sherman, the twins Christopher and Anthony, and I processed our own mixture of excitement and apprehension about leaving everything familiar for something unknown.

"How much farther?" became the regular question as the miles accumulated and the landscape changed from the familiar terrain of Alabama to the rolling hills of Georgia.

"We'll get there before dark," Horace said, knowing that children needed to know there was a destination and that this uncertain journey would soon come to an end.

The house Horace had purchased for the family was located on the northwest side of Atlanta, in an area called Grove Park. Their new home was close enough to walk downtown, but far enough from the city center to provide space for children to play safely. Like everything else about our new life, it represented possibilities that hadn't existed in Selma: more space, better schools, public recreation parks, libraries, and proximity to economic opportunities that could support the family's continued growth and development.

Although the house had two levels, the upper level had sustained fire that left the upstairs bedrooms unusable and desperately in need of immediate renovations for a family of eight children and two adults. Fortunately, Horace already had ideas of what was needed, and he'd long ago planned the remodeling that would make the lower level of the house and kitchen work for their immediate needs. His work would start at once, and all the boys would be busy learning carpentry and painting.

"This is going to be your home," he told the children, as we roamed around among empty rooms and tried to picture how we would use the space. "But it's also going to be your first job. Everybody is going to help turn this house into a place that we can enjoy and that works for our family."

The remodeling project became the family's introduction to Atlanta and to our new stepfather's approach to combining work and education. Horace understood that learning practical skills would serve the children well regardless of what careers we eventually pursued, and the house renovation provided opportunities for hands-on learning that complemented our formal education.

Under his direction, the boys learned how to take accurate measurements, use hand and power tools, operate electric saws safely, and measure, cut, and hang wallboard and paint like a pro. We learned that building was a mix of the grit of hard work and sound thinking, that the best work came out of thoughtful planning and focus on the details, and that at the end it took working together to get things done. Eventually, the older kids, including me, would be working with our stepfather on proper building jobs.

"Measure twice, cut once," became the household motto during the renovation period, but the lesson extended beyond carpentry to everything the family was learning about their new life in Atlanta. Careful planning and preparation were essential for success in unfamiliar circumstances.

Before the family's arrival, Horace had done thorough research to determine what grade schools and high schools would be best for the children to attend. Carrie was quite impressed by how he had demonstrated his commitment to ensuring that the children's academic development continued without interruption. Although he had found schools that would offer the same standard of education they had received at Saint Elizabeth, both schools would mean traveling across town rather than walking to the nearby neighborhood schools.

"For all of you going to high school, it's going to mean boarding a bus each morning and traveling to downtown, and from there catching a connection to Southwest Atlanta," he explained to Yolanda and Joan, who would be entering their final year of high school. "Initially, we'll drive you to school until you're familiar with the city and comfortable with the transportation system."

This setup was initially somewhat uncomfortable for all of the children, but they knew it reflected their mother's continued dedication to their education even when it became a matter of some extra trouble and expenditure. They also knew their parents were making sacrifices to provide them with the most extensive preparation for any opportunities they might pursue.

Frederick and I, who were entering our sophomore year in high school, would have three more years of high school in Atlanta. Sherman was about to enter the fifth grade, and Christopher and Anthony were starting fourth grade. Each child would have to adjust to new schools, new teachers, and new expectations while contending with what they had already learned at Saint Elizabeth.

It was a difficult but possible leap for all of us because we knew about adversity from those years in Selma. And the discipline, work habits, and confidence we developed through our Catholic education gave us a bolstering path to navigate unfamiliar academic environments and establish nurturing connections with teachers who didn't know our family's history or what we were mentally capable of achieving.

"Remember you are representing not just yourselves but everything you learned in Selma," Carrie reminded us as we prepared to start our first days at new schools. "Treat your teachers the same way you treated those nuns, work as hard as you've ever worked in your life at Saint Elizabeth's, and don't let anyone tell you that there is any place where you are unable to achieve."

The quick success we experienced at our new schools reaffirmed both the preparation we had done and our parents' faith in us. What became immediately apparent to educators was that these students were exceptional in some way, not only academically but also in terms of maturity and valuing education. Carrie's children believed that individual success wasn't simply a matter of accumulating impressive grades but was also a matter of being genuinely interested in their classmates' achievements as well.

Though she carried her medical instruments with her, Carrie left her midwifery practice behind. In later years she would work in assisted living facilities and in-home personal care, but she never returned to the full-fledged, community-based medical vocation she had maintained in Selma under Dr. Dumont. Horace's savings and the income he would soon earn were enough to sustain the family, so Carrie's early years in Atlanta were filled with family and household duties. While part of her always missed the purposeful feeling of bringing new life into the world and tending to the health of children and adults, she felt fulfilled in her more than two decades of service to her Selma neighborhood. And now she experienced the joy and security of her family's new life in Atlanta.

Carrie's example seeped into her children's lives in many ways, one of the dearest was Joan's vocational pursuits. Joan enrolled at Egleston Memorial Hospital School of Nursing immediately after graduating from high school, catching an early morning bus while it was still dark to begin the rigorous training that would prepare her to follow in her mother's footsteps. Her transition to nursing school demonstrated how the family's commitment to service continued even in their unfamiliar environment.

"I know it's still pretty dark in the mornings, so I'll walk with you to the bus stop until it's lighter earlier," I told my sister, understanding that the family's mutual support system needed to adapt to Atlanta's urban environment while maintaining the same principles that had governed our lives in Selma.

These walks to the bus stop in the mornings were time for conversation about what we were working toward, how we struggled, and what we were dealing with in adjusting to city life. We siblings would continue to encourage each other's educational and professional successes, just as we had learned to do at 1421 Sylvan Street.

The economic opportunities in Atlanta were evident from the moment we arrived and influenced the future prospects of the whole family. Horace's experience in construction and general contracting allowed him access to projects that would have been unavailable in Selma's smaller economy. The skills he'd acquired during his years in the Merchant Marine and on building projects around the world were easily transferred to a city that was expanding rapidly and needed already experienced contractors.

But more important still were the ways Atlanta's booming economy provided us children with an array of opportunities to dream about work and a future that stretched far beyond anything we had ever thought possible in Selma. The city was brimming with universities, beautiful public libraries, hospitals, industries, and cultural entities that meant possibilities of educational growth and professional paths.

"This city is going to afford all of you opportunities that you would not have had if we'd stayed in Selma," Carrie noted to her children as we discovered the resources available to us when we first encountered our new community. "But opportunities are nothing unless you're ready to work for them and use them wisely."

The family's commitment to service and community engagement found new expression in Atlanta's more diverse environment. While we had been part of a close-knit African American community in Selma, Atlanta exposed us to people from a variety of backgrounds, ethnicities, and experiences. The principles we had learned about treating everyone with dignity and respect proved universally applicable.

The cooking lessons that Carrie had begun in Selma continued in the larger kitchen in our Atlanta home, with all the children learning to prepare family meals and manage household responsibilities. The upside-down pineapple cake and banana pudding recipes that had been family favorites in Selma traveled well to Georgia, providing continuity and comfort during a period of considerable change.

"Some things don't change no matter where you live," Carrie said as she taught Sherman and the younger twins the same cooking techniques she had taught their older siblings. "Taking care of each other, sharing what you have, and making sure everyone feels loved and valued—those things are the same whether you're in Selma or Atlanta or anywhere else."

The self-reliance skills that had been necessary for survival in Selma proved equally valuable in Atlanta's more complex urban environment. The children's ability to sort, wash, and fold clothes, to prepare meals, to help younger siblings with homework, and to manage minor emergencies without adult supervision served us well as we adapted to new schedules and responsibilities.

A most notable aspect of the family's transition to Atlanta was how it proved the portability of the values and relationships that had sustained us in Selma. The mutual support, shared responsibility, and commitment to service that had accompanied us from when we roomed together in the house at 1421 Sylvan Street still continued to govern our lives in our new home.

"We're still the same family we were in Selma," Horace noted as he watched the children adapt to our unfamiliar environment while preserving the same caring relationships with each other. "We're just discovering what that family can do when presented with access to more opportunities."

In 1970, while the family was still settling into their new Atlanta life, both Carrie and Joan gave birth—baby Shelia Marie to Carrie and baby Jeffrey to Joan—beginning the next generation of children who would carry forward the family's commitment to service, achievement, and caring for others.

Carrie's parenting continued to evolve even into her later years. Shelia, born from Carrie's new union with Horace when Carrie was forty-three, experienced a different version of motherhood than the older children had—one shaped by experience, wisdom, and weariness, from decades of raising children.

"We did not always see eye-to-eye," Shelia would reflect, "but I had the absolute best mother that anyone could ever have had. By the time I came along, my mother Carrie was tired, but she still knew how to mother, and she was a good mother at that."

When conflicts arose during Shelia's teenage years, intense arguments between a mother who hadn't dealt with a teenager in years and a daughter asserting her independence would often reach an impasse. But Carrie found a solution that drew on her love of written communication and her understanding that sometimes the most important conversations required careful thought rather than heated words.

"What became an unusual but beautiful resolution to these often-uncomfortable arguments started one night after we had argued earlier that morning," Shelia remembered. "When I entered my room, there lay on the bed a sealed envelope that said 'Shelia' in beautiful cursive."

Inside was a letter from her mother explaining in loving detail what she wanted Shelia to understand, her concerns and hopes expressed with the same careful attention to communication that had shaped her correspondence with family members throughout her life. The letter opened a new channel of communication between mother and daughter.

"I returned my own thoughts in a letter as well," Shelia continued. "From that day on, we would always write resolving love letters to one another. She had such beautiful penmanship and expressed her feelings so earnestly. We had found our love language, and I loved communicating with her in this way."

This same gift for written communication had sustained Carrie's relationship with all her children as we moved into adulthood and established our own lives. When I was in college, her letters arrived regularly, with news from home, encouragement about my studies, and the kind of maternal wisdom that could only be fully appreciated with the maturing perspective that comes from time and distance.

The success of the transition to Atlanta validated Carrie's decision to remarry and relocate. Her children were thriving academically, developing new skills through the house renovation project, and beginning to envision futures that would make full use of our talents and preparation. The foundation laid in Selma was proving strong enough to support whatever they chose to build upon it.

By the end of our first year in Atlanta, the family had established new routines, new neighbors and friends, and new goals that incorporated the best of what we had brought from Selma with the expanded possibilities our new city offered. We were no longer simply Carrie's kids from Sylvan Street—we were young people prepared to contribute to whatever communities we chose to join and to carry forward the values of service, education, mutual support, and justice that had shaped our development.

The foundation was complete, the transition successful, and the future full of promise. The circle continued, the legacy was secure, and the story that had begun with Hettie Lundy on Saint Ann Street was finding new expression in a new city with new possibilities. Atlanta had indeed risen to provide the opportunities that would allow this remarkable family to fulfill the potential nurtured through years of love, discipline, and elevated expectations in a small house on a dirt road in Selma, Alabama.

EPILOGUE

The Sacred Memory of Sylvan Street

At the beach—All the children have grown a lot . . . To hear little feet running over the house sounds nice to hear early in the morning. They were all happy to see me.

—Carrie Louise, Jun. 24, 2001

It was a quiet Tuesday morning in 2011 when the phone rang and I learned the news I had been expecting—and dreading—for years. Mommie was gone. Carrie Louise Lundy Jones Hunter, age eighty-four, peacefully slipped into glory in her sleep. She was surrounded by the love that had defined her entire life, and she left behind a legacy that would continue to shape generations she would never meet.

Sitting in my own kitchen that morning, hundreds of miles from the small house on Sylvan Street where it all began, I found myself thinking not about loss but about abundance. The remarkable richness of Mommie's life had touched hundreds of families, delivered countless babies safely into the world, and raised ten children who had gone on to contribute their own gifts to communities far beyond Selma, Alabama.

The woman we had all called Mommie until the day she died had lived to see her children take up meaningful careers: a federal judge, an army sergeant, a registered nurse, an electrical engineer, a professional hair stylist, and business entrepreneurs. She had seen her grandchildren graduating from universities, pursuing advanced degrees, and establishing careers that built on the foundation of service and excellence she had laid decades earlier in a seven-room house surrounded by pecan trees and roses.

But far more important still, Carrie Louise lived to witness the values she held dear reflected in the lives of her children and grandchildren. She consistently treated every person with dignity, regardless of their background or circumstance. Her commitment to serving others was unwavering, and she never expected recognition or reward for her acts of kindness. Carrie, like her mother Hettie, believed deeply that personal achievement had little meaning unless it benefited the community at large. These ideals became the foundation upon which her family built their own lives. Through her example and guidance, she instilled these ideals in the next generations, ensuring that her legacy would endure as her children and grandchildren carried those values into their own work, relationships, and communities.

In the days following her passing, as family members gathered to share memories of Mommie and celebrate her life and influence, emerging stories painted a picture of a life we had not fully appreciated while she was alive. Former patients, now in their old age, had come to pay respects to the woman who had brought their babies into the world and given medical care when no one else was available. An Atlanta Jewish family spoke about Carrie's kindness and generosity during the years she had cared for their elderly mother. All the family loved her as a second mother.

Once, a woman I didn't recognize came up to me and said, "Your mother saved my life." She introduced herself as someone Carrie had helped through a difficult pregnancy in the 1950s. "But more than that, she made me feel like I mattered, like my baby mattered, like our family deserved the same quality of care that anyone else would receive."

These kinds of conversations brought to mind something I had started to realize only as an adult—Carrie's work as a nurse and midwife, along with the labor of countless Black women of her generation, had been indispensable but would never appear in official history. She had kept families alive and healthy, helped women through their most vulnerable times, and delivered medical care that often made the difference between life and death. But her name would never be printed in medical textbooks or history books about healthcare in the American South.

Our father's service in the military, like so much of what Carrie and others contributed, had gone unacknowledged for decades.

Clarence Sr. passed on in 1971, long before his country received the memo about what he'd contributed in service. He'd driven ammunition trucks through war-torn Europe, worn the uniform, put himself at great risk—and then returned home to Jim Crow. It just ranked for him in the list of things he had done with his life, like cutting a Christmas tree or painting a house, none of which was really worth trumpeting. He had lived his life, raised his family (until his departure for Cleveland and his premature death left Carrie to finish out that work alone) and, died without any official recognition for what he'd accomplished during the war.

It wasn't unique. There are countless Black veterans who did not get that type of recognition, no sense of honor or acknowledgment for their service. The system rendered the service they provided—and so much of Black life and work—invisible: Carrie's midwifery, our family's involvement in civil rights, and thousands of community members who were keeping the movement going.

In fact, it wouldn't be until years after Clarence Sr.'s death, and only after a direct order from President Barack Obama that all veterans whose service went unacknowledged be acknowledged, that our oldest sister Gwendolyn asked for and received a Presidential Memorial Certificate in memory of our father.

The certificate, provided by the U.S. Department of Veterans Affairs, states: "The United States of America honors the memory of Clarence Jones Sr. This certificate of service is presented by a grateful

Nation in appreciation for your many years of faithful and dedicated service to the United States."

Better late than never, perhaps. But the delay has its own virtues, telling a story about who is remembered and who is forgotten, about whose service counts and whose goes unseen, about the generations-long battle we have fought for recognition that marks not only our father's military experience but our family's history as well.

When I consider that certificate arriving decades after Daddy died, I think about all the other acknowledgments that arrived too late or not at all:

Carrie's decades of providing midwifery, done only in secret as Jim Crow laws restricted who could practice officially.

The many neighbors and thousands of community members who fed, housed, and supported civil rights workers—whose names appear in no history books.

The children who marched—my siblings, cousins, and I were among them—are largely untold in many of the histories of the movement.

The mothers who made the often-agonizing decision to let their children put everything on the line, including our mother, Carrie, whose courage in letting us participate deserves just as much praise as any medal of valor.

This book is, in some sense, my own equivalent to Gwendolyn's request for Daddy's certificates. It's a reminder that our family's service—in war and the struggle for civil rights—should be remembered. That our mother be recognized for her bravery. That the friends on whom we relied not be forgotten. That the children who marched be recognized as participants, not simply observers.

My father fought in Europe so that freedom could defeat fascism. Decades later, his children would help open the gates of Selma to freedom. Both were of service to our country, whether formally acknowledged or not.

Carrie's heroism was undocumented except in family memories, birth records, and the quiet gratitude of people whose lives had been touched by her skill and compassion. She belonged to a generation of

African American women whose daily acts of service sustained their communities through segregation and beyond, whose work was crucial but rarely recognized beyond the families they directly served.

As I reflected on her life and legacy, I found myself thinking about the larger context of what she had accomplished. The Catholic mission to Selma's Black community—including Dr. Dumont, Ms. Joan Mulder, the Sisters of Saint Joseph, the Edmundite Priests and Brothers—had provided opportunities and resources that wouldn't have existed otherwise. But it had required someone like Carrie to translate those opportunities into enduring change for individual families and the broader community.

The teamwork between Dr. Dumont and Carrie went beyond a strictly working relationship. It was a partnership in the full sense of the word, rooted in shared values and complementary strengths. Both women understood that healing extended beyond the realm of clinical expertise; it required compassion, empathy, and a heartfelt respect for the life experiences of those they served. Their collaboration showed that when it came to working with marginalized communities, sensitivity and cultural fluency—not just technical know-how—had the power to bridge trust and communication gaps. Together, Dr. Dumont and Carrie were united in building a legacy for the future by investing in education to ensure that change would be generational.

The house at 1421 Sylvan Street, which Dr. Dumont had helped them purchase, had become exactly what it was intended to be—not just a family home but a community resource where medical care, childcare, spiritual support, and practical assistance flowed naturally together. It had been a place where children learned by watching that service to others was life's highest calling, and where neighbors found the kind of comprehensive support that helped families thrive even under difficult circumstances.

But the most remarkable aspect of Carrie's legacy was how she had prepared her children for opportunities that didn't yet exist when they were growing up. The education she had secured for them at Saint Elizabeth, the confidence she had instilled through her parenting philosophy, and the values she had modeled through her daily service had shaped young people who could excel in whatever environment they encountered.

Her decision to allow her children to participate in the civil rights movement, despite the risks such participation entailed, demonstrated wisdom that went far beyond conventional parenting advice. She had understood that shielding children from moral challenges would leave them unprepared for moral responsibilities, and courage was something that had to be chosen freely rather than imposed from outside.

The results spoke for themselves. Her children had become leaders in their respective fields, contributors to their communities, and parents who passed on the same values of service and excellence to the next generation. They had fulfilled the potential she had seen in them. More importantly, they had used their success to create opportunities for others who needed help.

The sacred memory of Sylvan Street wasn't just about one remarkable woman or one extraordinary family; it was about the power of communities to nurture potential, the importance of investing in children's futures, and the way individual acts of service can create ripple effects that extend far beyond their immediate circumstances.

The small house surrounded by a chain-link fence and pink roses, the daily walks to Saint Elizabeth Catholic School, the midnight calls to deliver babies, the pea shelling parties that brought neighbors together—all these ordinary moments had been building something extraordinary. A family that would contribute to changing American society, a set of values that would influence generations, and a demonstration that excellence and service could flourish even under the most challenging circumstances.

As I stood in the cemetery in Atlanta where Mommie was laid to rest, surrounded by children, grandchildren, great-grandchildren, nieces, and nephews whose very existence testified to the success of her life's work, I realized that the story that had begun with Hettie Lundy on Saint Ann Street was continuing in ways that none of us could fully predict or control.

Horace Hunter, whom the children would eventually call "Pops," now 104 years old, continues to live in Austin, Texas, with Shelia and her husband, his mind still sharp and his presence a living link to the maritime adventures that brought him into Carrie's life. Shelia, the daughter he and Carrie had together in 1970, had become a successful hair stylist serving celebrities, while creating Carrie Louise Designs—a fashion brand that honored her mother's creativity and diligence. Joan's son Jeffrey, born the same year and now a high school teacher and athletic coach, grew up to embody the same commitment to service that characterized his grandmother's approach to life.

Carrie's legacy was secure not because it was preserved in monuments or official records, but because it had been embedded in the character and values of people who continued to serve others, to pursue excellence, and to believe that individual success meant nothing without collective advancement.

The sacred memory of Sylvan Street would live on not in the physical location—though the house still stands, now occupied by other families pursuing their own dreams—but in the principles and practices that had been learned there and carried forward into new communities, new careers, and new challenges.

Standing there in the Atlanta sunshine, thinking about the journey that had brought us from a dirt road in Selma to opportunities and achievements that would have seemed impossible in 1947, I understood something I hadn't fully grasped while Mommie was living. Her greatest achievement hadn't been any individual accomplishment—not the babies she had delivered, not the patients she had healed, not even the children she had raised to success.

Her greatest achievement had been demonstrating that ordinary people could accomplish extraordinary things when they combined love with discipline, service with excellence, and individual achievement with collective responsibility. She had shown that it was possible to build a life of significance even under the most limiting circumstances, and that the most important legacy anyone could leave was children and communities prepared to continue the work of making the world more just, more compassionate, and more welcoming for everyone.

The sacred memory of Sylvan Street was about possibility; the possibility that love could triumph over hatred, that service could create lasting change, that children raised with high expectations and unlimited support could exceed everyone's dreams of what they might accomplish.

That possibility was now real in the life of one remarkable woman and the family she had created. Now it was up to the rest of us to ensure that the same possibility remained available to future generations who would face their own challenges and discover their own opportunities to serve something larger than themselves.

The story was complete, but the legacy would continue for as long as people were willing to believe that individual acts of love and service could change the world, one family at a time. •

Acknowledgments

This book exists because of countless acts of love, courage, and support across three generations. Thanks to all of you.

To my mother, Carrie Louise Lundy, whose "raised to fly" philosophy gave nine children wings strong enough to carry us through history. Every page testifies to your radical trust, your unwavering belief in our capabilities, and your refusal to clip our wings even when the world was a dangerous place.

To my grandmother, Hettie Lundy, whose wisdom formed the foundation on which Carrie built. Your life lessons live on these pages and in all of your grandchildren.

To my father, Clarence Jones Sr., whose story reminds us that systemic forces are real and often defeat even the most devoted hearts. Your service and struggle deserve to be remembered with love, understanding, and compassion.

To my siblings—Gwendolyn, Carolyn, Yolanda, Joan, Frederick, Sherman, Christopher, Anthony, and Shelia—who all shared this journey. Special thanks to Gwendolyn for being our family historian and always bringing the stories that only she could tell. To Frederick, my twin, for walking the streets of Selma with me and through every moment documented here.

To the Sisters of Saint Joseph and ***the Edmundite Priests and Brothers*** at Saint Elizabeth Catholic School and Church, whose dedication to educating Black children in segregated Alabama prepared us for lives of service and civic engagement. You were hidden heroes of the movement.

To Dr. Isabelle Dumont, who provided my mother with stable employment and became a pillar of our community's health and survival.

To the community members who sustained us—Mrs. Willie Mae Dawson, Mrs. Tena, Ms. Emma, the neighbors who provided childcare, our country relatives who brought food and the members of Brown

Chapel AME Church and Green Street Baptist—who created networks of mutual aid. You prove that movements are built on daily acts of community care and kindness.

To Uncle Sylvester "DeeDee" Lundy and all our uncles, whose love and laughter filled our childhood, and whose presence on Selma's front lines showed us that courage and joy could coexist.

To the civil rights leaders who organized in Selma—Dr. Martin Luther King Jr., Dr. Ralph Abernathy, John Lewis, Reverend Hosea Williams, James Bevel, Diane Nash, and countless others—who trusted that children and families could be active participants in the movement for justice.

To my editor, VanDunk Edits, whose patient guidance shaped this manuscript from family memory into coherent narrative. This book is immeasurably better for your collaboration.

To Garon Hart, whose design transforms these stories into a beautiful volume, including the family album and book cover.

To my wife and children, who have always supported my work and obsession with completing a project.

To Dr. Keyser and Howard University, who inspired me to write and enabled my education and discipline, which equipped me for this work.

To the readers, educators, and students who will engage with this book: Thank you for honoring these stories. May Carrie's "raised to fly" philosophy inspire you to prepare the next generation not by protecting them from challenge, but by building in them the courage to meet it.

Finally, *to all the mothers who made impossible choices during impossible times*, to all the children who marched, to all the communities who sustained families through both survival and revolution—this book is for you.

The civil rights movement wasn't built only by famous leaders. It was built by ordinary people who decided justice was worth the risk. This is their story. This is our story.

About the Author

Born in Selma, Alabama in 1953, Clarence is the eldest son of Carrie Louise Lundy. He grew up at 1421 Sylvan Street, three blocks from Brown Chapel AME Church, where civil rights mass meetings in the early 1960s planned the activities that would change America.

At age twelve, Clarence participated in both Selma to Montgomery marches, including the violence of Bloody Sunday on March 7, 1965. He attended Saint Elizabeth Catholic School, taught by the Sisters of Saint Joseph—missionary nuns dedicated to educating Black children in the segregated South. For nine years, he served as an altar boy, learning the pre-Vatican II Latin Mass and the discipline of ritual. His mother, though remaining faithful to her own Baptist tradition, chose this Catholic education for her children, valuing the rigorous spiritual and academic formation it provided.

After the family relocated to Atlanta in 1968, Clarence earned his BS in Electrical Engineering from Howard University. He built a successful career as an electrical systems engineer and technical writer in automation, software, and IT Industries. Having authored several technical titles, *Carrie's Children* is his first literary work, bringing an engineer's precision to documenting how his mother's extraordinary parenting made history possible and mattered as much as the marches themselves.

Author on Memories and Recollections

Reconstructing History from a Child's Perspective

This memoir documents events I experienced between ages ten and twelve, now seen through six decades of distance. Readers understandably ask: How can you remember such specific details from childhood? First, I'd say that I've always had a good memory for things that happened, and both good memories and traumatic memories are long-lasting.

Some memories burn themselves into consciousness and never fade. I can still smell and feel the sting of teargas. I can still see the chaotic running and the felled bodies on the Edmund Pettus Bridge. I can still hear Hosea Williams's voice at mass meetings, and hum along in my mind. I can still see my mother pedaling at her sewing machine, and patterns spread about. Selma, indeed, is quite unforgettable.

These memories remained vivid as our family talked of them, often around our dinner table on Sylvan Street, throughout the years. Even later in Atlanta after 1968, we would sometimes reconstruct events. My eight siblings and I compared perspectives, corrected recollections, and filled gaps in each other's memories. My mother, Carrie, provided the adult context we'd failed to comprehend as children.

Beyond family memory, I've verified events through historical documentation: contemporary newspapers, movement archives, published histories, documentary footage, and photographs—including the March 19, 1965, *Time Magazine* cover capturing our uncle Sylvester "DeeDee" Lundy front and center.

From early on, as an engineer and technical writer, I have always valued precision and documentation. When I recreate dialogue, specifically, I'm rendering the substance, the scene, and the tone of conversations as accurately as memory and family corroboration allow—not verbatim transcripts, but truthful representations of what was said.

Memory has limits. Where I've been unsure, I've said so. Where my siblings remember differently, I've acknowledged alternative perspectives. Where documentation contradicts recollection, I've deferred to the historical record.

What I can verify absolutely are the locations, major events, presence of specific leaders, timeline, family decisions, and emotional truth of what we experienced. I was there. My family was there. When you're a family of ten, most scenes and events are cemented into memory.

This book represents my best effort to honor our experience with the accuracy it deserves: the precision of an engineer applied to preserving memory, the clarity of a technical writer applied to making history accessible, and the honesty of a son determined to tell his mother's story as it happened.

The details matter. Carrie Louise Lundy and her children matter. The hidden heroes, the mothers, neighbors, and teachers who sustained both daily life and the courage that made their children foot soldiers all deserve documentation as carefully as that given to adult participants.

This memoir is my contribution to ensuring that their stories don't disappear.

Selected Bibliography

A Guide to Further Reading

This memoir emerges from an era in which a rich body of civil rights literature has developed. For readers interested in learning more, I recommend the following works.

Civil Rights Movement - Adult Leaders' Perspectives

Branch, Taylor. *Parting the Waters: America in the King Years, 1954–1963*. New York: Simon & Schuster, 1988.

Lewis, John, with Michael D'Orso. *Walking with the Wind: A Memoir of the Movement*. New York: Simon & Schuster, 1998.

King, Martin Luther Jr. *Why We Can't Wait*. New York: Harper & Row, 1964.

Civil Rights Movement - Youth and Women's Perspectives

Beals, Melba Pattillo. *Warriors Don't Cry: A Searing Memoir of the Battle to Integrate Little Rock's Central High*. New York: Pocket Books, 1994.

Webb, Sheyann, and Rachel West Nelson. *Selma, Lord, Selma: Girlhood Memories of the Civil Rights Days*. Tuscaloosa: University of Alabama Press, 1980.

Lewis, John, Andrew Aydin, and Nate Powell. *March* (trilogy). Marietta, GA: Top Shelf Productions, 2013–2016.

Olson, Lynne. *Freedom's Daughters: The Unsung Heroines of the Civil Rights Movement from 1830 to 1970*. New York: Scribner, 2001.

McGuire, Danielle L. *At the Dark End of the Street: Black Women, Rape, and Resistance*. New York: Knopf, 2010.

Selma-Specific History

Fager, Charles E. *Selma, 1965: The March That Changed the South*. New York: Scribner, 1974.

Garrow, David J. *Protest at Selma: Martin Luther King, Jr., and the Voting Rights Act of 1965*. New Haven: Yale University Press, 1978.

Black Catholic History

Davis, Cyprian. *The History of Black Catholics in the United States.* New York: Crossroad, 1990.

Massingale, Bryan N. *Racial Justice and the Catholic Church.* Maryknoll, NY: Orbis Books, 2010.

Community Organizing and Social Movements

Payne, Charles M. *I've Got the Light of Freedom: The Organizing Tradition and the Mississippi Freedom Struggle.* Berkeley: University of California Press, 1995.

Ransby, Barbara. *Ella Baker and the Black Freedom Movement: A Radical Democratic Vision.* Chapel Hill: University of North Carolina Press, 2003.

For Young Readers

Levinson, Cynthia. *We've Got a Job: The 1963 Birmingham Children's March.* Atlanta: Peachtree Publishers, 2012.

Partridge, Elizabeth. *Marching for Freedom: Walk Together, Children, and Don't You Grow Weary.* New York: Viking, 2009.

Documentary Films

Eyes on the Prize: America's Civil Rights Years (1987, PBS) - Episode 6 covers Selma

Selma: The Bridge to the Ballot (2015, Smithsonian Channel)

Selma (2014, dir. Ava DuVernay) - Feature film dramatization

Archives and Museums

National Voting Rights Museum and Institute, Selma, AL - www.nvrmi.com

National Park Service: Selma to Montgomery National Historic Trail - www.nps.gov/semo

Birmingham Civil Rights Institute - www.bcri.org

Timeline of Key Events

The Jones Family and the Selma Movement

1945-1950s: Foundation

1945 - Clarence Jones Sr. serves in WWII as ammunition truck driver

July 22, 1946 - Clarence Sr. marries Carrie Louise Lundy

1947 - Gwendolyn Jones, first of ten children, born to Carrie Louise Lundy

1953 - Clarence T. Jones born in Selma, Alabama

1953 – Late 1950s - Jones family at 1421 Sylvan Street; children attend Saint Elizabeth Catholic School

1954 - *Brown v. Board of Education* decision

1960-1963: Organizing Begins

1963 - "Freedom Day" voter registration in Selma; Clarence begins altar boy service

May 1963 - Clarence accidentally attends first mass meeting at Tabernacle Baptist Church

1964 - Civil Rights Act signed; SNCC and SCLC increase Selma organizing

1965: The Turning Point

January 1965 - Dr. King joins Selma campaign; mass meetings intensify at Brown Chapel; Jones children begin attending

February 1965 - Continued protests; Jimmie Lee Jackson shot February 18, die February 26

March 7, 1965 - **Bloody Sunday** - 600 marchers including Clarence (age 12) attacked at Edmund Pettus Bridge; footage broadcast nationally

March 9, 1965 - Dr. King leads "Turnaround Tuesday"; Rev. James Reeb attacked, dies March 11

March 19, 1965 - *Time Magazine* cover features Uncle Sylvester "DeeDee" Lundy next to John Lewis

March 21-25, 1965 – Selma to Montgomery March

Jones children and 3,200 marchers depart, grow to 25,000

March 24, 1965 - The Night the 'Stars' Came Out in Alabama

March 25, 1965 - King's "How Long, Not Long" speech at Alabama Capitol; Viola Liuzzo murdered that night

August 6, 1965 - Voting Rights Act signed into law

1966-Present: Aftermath and Legacy

1968 - Jones family relocates to Atlanta

1970s - Clarence earns BSEE, Howard University

1980s-2020s - Career as engineer and technical writer

March 2026 - Publication of *Carrie's Children*

Key Locations

1421 Sylvan Street - Jones family home

Brown Chapel Church - Selma Movement headquarters

Saint Elizabeth Catholic School - Where the children were educated

Edmund Pettus Bridge - Site of Bloody Sunday

Dallas County Courthouse - Voter registration/protest site

About the Organizations

Key Institutions in the Selma Movement

SCLC - Southern Christian Leadership Conference

Founded in 1957 by Dr. King and other ministers after the Montgomery Bus Boycott. SCLC coordinated nonviolent campaigns across the South, emphasizing moral authority of the Black church. In January 1965, SCLC joined SNCC's Selma organizing, bringing national attention and leaders including King, Hosea Williams, Andrew Young, and James Bevel. SCLC led the mass meetings at Brown Chapel that the Jones children attended.

SNCC - Student Nonviolent Coordinating Committee

Founded 1960 by young activists including John Lewis and Diane Nash. SNCC pioneered grassroots organizing and local leadership development. SNCC workers began organizing Selma in early 1963, establishing voter registration and community infrastructure before SCLC's involvement. SNCC emphasized empowering local people—like the Jones family—to take direct action.

Brown Chapel AME Church

Under Pastor L. L. Anderson, Brown Chapel at 410 Martin Luther King Jr. Street served as the movement headquarters, hosting mass meetings and serving as a gathering point for marches. Its location, three blocks from the Jones' home, made participation logistically possible for young people. The church still stands as part of Selma to Montgomery National Historic Trail.

Saint Elizabeth Catholic Mission (School)

Catholic school serving Selma's Black community, staffed by the Sisters of Saint Joseph. Combined rigorous academics with Catholic Social Teaching emphasizing human dignity, service, and justice. All nine Jones children attended, learning pre-Vatican II Latin Mass and receiving formation that prepared them for civic participation.

Sisters of Saint Joseph

Catholic missionary nuns (Missionary Servants of the Most Blessed Trinity) dedicated to serving African American communities in the segregated South. They taught the Jones children not just academics but dignity, discipline, and the imperative to serve others—lessons that carried directly into civil rights participation.

Dallas County Voters League

Local Black organization founded by Amelia Boynton, Marie Foster, and others. Organized citizenship classes, voter registration, and community mobilization before national organizations arrived—the grassroots foundation that made later work possible.

National Voting Rights Museum and Institute

Located in Selma (1012 Water Avenue), preserves voting rights struggle history and honors participants. Collects oral histories, artifacts, and documentation.

For More Information

National Park Service: Selma to Montgomery National Historic Trail - www.nps.gov/semo

National Voting Rights Museum - www.nvrmi.com

Brown Chapel AME Church - 410 Martin Luther King Jr. Street (formerly Sylvan Street), Selma, AL 36701

www.ingramcontent.com/pod-product-compliance
Lightning Source LLC
Chambersburg PA
CBHW032015050726
47590CB00006B/2188

* 9 7 8 1 8 8 9 1 0 1 1 5 6 *